The Brothers Karamazov

WORLDS OF THE NOVEL

Twayne's Masterwork Studies

Robert Lecker, *General Editor*

The Brothers Karamazov

WORLDS OF THE NOVEL

Robin Feuer Miller

TWAYNE PUBLISHERS • NEW YORK
Maxwell Macmillan Canada • Toronto
Maxwell Macmillan International • New York Oxford Singapore Sydney

Twayne's Masterwork Studies No. 83

The Brothers Karamazov: Worlds of the Novel
Robin Feuer Miller

Twayne Publishers
Macmillan Publishing Company
866 Third Avenue
New York, New York 10022

Maxwell Macmillan Canada, Inc.
1200 Eglinton Avenue East
Suite 200
Don Mills, Ontario M3C 3N1

Macmillan Publishing Company is part of the Maxwell Communication
Group of Companies.

Library of Congress Cataloging-in-Publication Data

Miller, Robin Feuer, 1947–
    The brothers Karamazov : worlds of the novels / Robin Feuer Miller.
      p.   cm.—(Twayne's masterwork studies ; no. 83)
    Includes bibliographical references and index.
    ISBN 0-8057-8060-2 (alk. paper)—ISBN 0-8057-8118-8
(pbk. : alk. paper)
    1. Dostoyevsky, Fyodor, 1821–1881.   Brat ´ia Karamazovy.
I. Title. II. Series.
PG3325.B73M7 1992
891.73´3—dc20   91-34020
                                                        CIP

The paper used in this publication meets the minimum requirements
of American National Standard for Information Sciences—Permanence
of Paper for Printed Library Materials. ANSI Z39.48-1984.⊗™

10 9 8 7 6 5 4 3 2 1 (hc)
10 9 8 7 6 5 4 3 2 1 (pb)

Printed in the United States of America

For my mother and father, Kathryn and Lewis Feuer,
and
for Lulu

Contents

Note on the References and Acknowledgments viii
Chronology of Fyodor Dostoevsky's Life and Work xi

Literary and Historical Context

   1. Historical Context 1
   2. The Importance of *The Brothers Karamazov* 4
   3. Critical Reception 7

A Reading

   4. Of Prefaces, Preludes, and Parodies 13
      Part I: Books I, II, and III

   5. The Deep Heart's Core 48
      Part II: Books IV, V, and VI

   6. The Plot Quickens 80
      Part III: Books VII, VIII, and IX

   7. Varieties of Guilty Experience 99
      Part IV: Books X, XI, XII, and the Epilogue

Notes 134
Selected Bibliography 139
Index 149

Note on the References and Acknowledgments

All page references to *The Brothers Karamazov* are to the Norton Critical Edition, translated by Constance Garnett and revised by Ralph E. Matlaw (New York: W. W. Norton and Company, 1976). Readers able to read Russian who want a handy cross-reference to the novel in the original Russian should consult Victor Terras's invaluable *A Karamazov Companion: Commentary on the Genesis, Language, and Style of Dostoevsky's Novel* (Madison: University of Wisconsin Press, 1981). This work contains notes and page references to both the Norton edition and the authoritative *Polnoe sobranie sochinenii v tridsati tomakh* (*Complete Works in Thirty Volumes*) (volumes 14 and 15), still appearing under the general editorship of G. M. Fridlender. Wherever possible I have referred to English translations of Russian primary and secondary materials.

I am particularly indebted in shaping my own reading of *The Brothers Karamazov* to the written work and the keen editorial sensibility of Robert L. Belknap. His remarkable courses on Dostoevsky at Columbia University have inspired several generations of students, many of whom have gone on to work on Dostoevsky themselves.

I wish also to thank the following friends and colleagues whose good advice I have greatly valued: Terri Artman, Sergei Belov, Diana L. Burgin, Ellen Chances, Caryl Emerson, Edward Engelberg, Victor Erlich, Donald Fanger, Galina Galagan, George Gibian, David Gordon, Jane Hale, Robert Louis Jackson, Mary Lou Leppert, John Malmstad, Ruth Murray Mathewson, Gary Saul Morson, Robert Szulkin, William Mills Todd III, Igor Volgin, Peggy Wiesenberg, Ellen Witherell, and Vladimir Zakharov. The curators of the Dostoevsky Museum in Staraya Russa enabled me to take the photographs in this book. I wish to thank both the director of the museum, Vera Bogdanova, and her assistant,

Note on the References and Acknowledgments

Natalia Shmeleva. Barbara Campbell's friendship is a rock, her artistic vision an inspiration. I owe Anne Janowitz particular thanks. And I thank Katherine T. O'Connor, in whom the boundaries of friend and colleague are intermingled and indistinguishable.

Brandeis University kindly supplied me with a fine computer, a quiet office, and a Mazer grant. The Harvard Russian Research Center offered continued support and, by its ongoing sponsorship of its seminars in Russian literature, important inspiration and a context for the exchange of ideas. The Marine Biological Laboratories of Woods Hole, Massachusetts, came to the rescue when DOS nearly devoured Dostoevsky.

My daughters, Abigail, Alexa, and Louisa, patiently accepted my preoccupation with those boys Kolya and Ilyusha.

Most of all, I wish to thank Christopher Miller for his help and for inspiring me to imitate his own energy, perseverance, and good cheer even when the present threatened to overwhelm the future.

The last photograph of Fyodor Dostoevsky.
From the Dostoevsky Museum in St. Petersburg

Chronology:
Fyodor Dostoevsky's Life and Work

1821   On 30 October Fyodor Mikhailovich Dostoevsky is born, the second son of Mikhail Andreevich Dostoevsky, a doctor at the Mariinsky Hospital in Moscow. The impact upon Dostoevsky of his stern father has been a subject of much conjecture. His beloved mother, Maria Fyodorovna, who frequently read him stories as a young child, helped shape his literary sensibility.

1831   Dr. Dostoevsky purchases a small provincial estate in Tula, where the young Dostoevsky spends time until he returns to Moscow, unwillingly, with his father to attend school in Moscow (1834).

1837   The great Russian poet Aleksandr Pushkin dies. Dostoevsky's mother dies. Dostoevsky is placed in an engineering preparatory school.

1838   Obeying his father, Dostoevsky enters the Academy of Military Engineering in St. Petersburg, despite his literary ambitions. Reads avidly, especially the works of Hoffmann, Balzac, and Hugo.

1839   Dostoevsky's father dies in June, probably the victim of murder by his own serfs. Dostoevsky, despite his active correspondence, remains largely silent about this event.

1843   Graduates from the Academy of Military Engineering and enters government service in St. Petersburg. Continues to be an avid reader of Russian and European literature.

1844   Resigns from his position to pursue a literary career. Completes his translation of Balzac's *Eugènie Grandet* (1833).

1846   Publishes *Poor Folk*. The story surrounding Dostoevsky's debut as a writer is a famous one in Russian literary history. The great Russian critic Vissarion Belinsky hails Dostoevsky as a major new writer and hopes he will prove to be a leading light of the Natural School. Dostoevsky enjoys a brief period as a member of Belinsky's pleiad, until his second work, *The Double* (1846), appears. Belinsky does not approve of the fantastic nature of this work. ("The fantastic in our time can have a place only in the lunatic asylum, not in literature.") Dostoevsky's brief term of literary lionization is over. He also publishes "Mr. Prokharchin."

Publishes "A Petersburg Chronicle" and "The Landlady." Begins his association with the Petrashevsky Circle.

Publishes "A Faint Heart," "An Honest Thief," "A Christmas Tree and a Wedding," "Another Man's Wife and the Husband under the Bed," and the deeply romantic portrait of a dreamer, *White Nights*. Affected by the revolutions of 1848 in Europe, Dostoevsky joins a secret society within the Petrashevsky Circle led by Nikolai Speshnev. This group plans to set up a secret printing press to publish pamphlets inciting the peasants to revolt.

Writes *Netochka Nezvanova*. Is arrested for his participation in the Petrashevsky Circle and spends the next year in solitary confinement in the Peter and Paul Fortress. He is tried, sentenced, and led to what he thinks will be his place of execution. But the czar has planned a cruel mock execution instead, and at the last moment Dostoevsky's sentence is commuted to four years of prison and a period of army service as a soldier in the ranks. He travels by sled and in irons to Siberia where he serves as a convict in Omsk. During this period in prison Dostoevsky reads the New Testament.

Serves in a battalion in Semipalatinsk, Siberia, and falls in love with Maria Dmitrievna Isaeva, the wife of a friend. Upon leaving prison, he asks his brother to send him Charles Dickens's *David Copperfield* (1849–50).

Anonymously publishes "A Little Hero" and marries Maria Dmitrievna, who had been widowed in 1855.

Publishes "Uncle's Dream" and *The Village of Stepanchikovo and Its Inhabitants*. At last receives permission to return to St. Petersburg. The radical and liberal community is ready to offer him a returning hero's welcome, but it is clear that his views have changed over the past decade. Critics like Nikolai Chernyshevsky and Nikolai Dobroliubov are eager to rediscover the social critic Dostoevsky, but he has returned from Siberia a deeply religious man who can no longer accept at face value the prescriptions of socialism.

1861   With his brother Mikhail, founds the successful journal *Time* and in it continues publishing his fictionalized prison memoir, *Notes from the House of the Dead* (1860–62). (The first four chapters appeared in Sept. 1860, in the journal *Russian World.*) Also publishes *The Insulted and Injured,* a novel deeply influenced by *The Old Curiosity Shop* (1840–41) by Charles Dickens. His marriage becomes increasingly unhappy. Also publishes in *Time* numerous articles reflecting his views on art and on the path that, in his view, should be taken by Russian literature. Particularly interesting are two entries, "Pedantry and Literacy" and "Mr.——bov and the Question of Art." In these articles Dostoevsky affirms the capacity of the peasants, once they have attained literacy, for appreciating great art. He sneers at art that resembles "copybook maxims."

1862–63   Makes his first trip abroad. Consults Parisian doctors about his epilepsy and visits Aleksandr Herzen in London. Expresses his often negative thoughts about this trip in *Winter Notes on Summer Impressions* (1863). During this period *Time* is ordered to halt publication by government censors, and Dostoevsky and his brother are financially wounded. This is also the period of his affair with Apollinaria Suslova, an affair that, on her side at least, cools quite quickly. With his brother, prepares for the publication of a second journal, *Epoch.*

1864   Publishes *Notes from Underground* in *Epoch.* His wife dies from tuberculosis. Mikhail Dostoevsky also dies suddenly, and Dostoevsky takes on the crushing burden of his brother's debts.

1865   Financial collapse of *Epoch.* Dostoevsky, desperate for funds, signs a contract with a ruthless publisher, Fyodor Stellovsky, in which he promises to give over all the rights of his future works if he does not publish a novel for Stellovsky within six months. Travels with his advance from Stellovsky to Europe, to the roulette tables of Wiesbaden. Loses heavily and asks both Ivan Turgenev and Aleksandr Herzen for loans—a humiliating act from which, especially vis-à-vis Turgenev, he never quite recovers. Plans for the first of his great "unwritten novels," *The Drunkards,* which eventually becomes one of the sources for *Crime and Punishment.* Returns to Petersburg in October. Begins his long association with Mikhail Katkov, the editor of the *Russian Herald.*

1866	Begins publication in the *Russian Herald* of *Crime and Punishment*. Meanwhile, honors his previous commitment to Stellovsky by presenting him with the novel, *The Gambler*. To finish this work on time, takes on the services of a young stenographer, Anna Grigorievna Snitkina, to whom he dictates the novel. Proposes marriage to her and continues thereafter to dictate his novels and stories to her.
1867	Marries Anna Grigorievna. She proves to be a steadfast, loyal, loving wife who manages over time to create an atmosphere of security in which Dostoevsky can work. They travel to Western Europe. While abroad, he writes *The Idiot* (1868) and *The Possessed* (1871; also called *The Devils* in some translations). His epilepsy worsens, and he continues to suffer occasionally from bouts of gambling.
1868	A baby, Sonya, is born in Geneva and lives for only three months. Dostoevsky continues work on *The Idiot*, which he completes during an eight-month stay in Florence. Plans another of his unwritten novels, *Atheism*.
1869	Another daughter, Lyubov, is born in Dresden. Dostoevsky reads about the murder of a student in Moscow by a radical group organized by Sergei Nechaev. He draws on this incident to create his novel *The Possessed*. Meanwhile, he begins to plan his last and greatest unwritten novel, *The Life of a Great Sinner*.
1870	Publishes *The Eternal Husband*. The shape of *The Possessed* begins to change from that of a political pamphlet to that of a complex, full-fledged novel.
1871	Begins publication of *The Possessed* in the *Russian Herald*. Takes great interest in the events surrounding the Paris Commune. The newspaper accounts of the ongoing trial of Nechaev provide continuing inspiration as he works on *The Possessed*. Decides to return to Russia. Burns the manuscripts of *The Idiot*, *The Eternal Husband* and *The Possessed*. Shortly after his return to Russia, Dostoevsky's son Fyodor is born.
1872	With his family, spends the summer in the country town of Staraya Russa, where they will continue to spend summers and which forms a source for the fictional town in which *The Brothers Karamazov* takes place. Becomes editor of the conservative journal *The Citizen*, in which he writes a weekly column entitled *The Diary of a Writer*.
1872–74	Anna Grigorievna manages to bring the family's financial affairs into good order and takes on the publication and distribu-

	tion of Dostoevsky's writings. Finds himself increasingly at odds with the conservative publishers of *The Citizen*.
1874	Travels to Bad Ems and to Geneva.
1875	Begins publication of his novel *A Raw Youth* in Nikolai Nekrasov's liberal journal, *Notes of the Fatherland*. His renewed friendly relations with Nekrasov lead to a cooling of his friendships with the more conservative Nikolai Strakhov and Apollon Maikov, who misunderstand Dostoevsky's point of view. They misread his desire for a sympathetic dialogue with the radicals as a turning toward radical beliefs. In August a son, Alexey, is born. Dostoevsky begins to publish *The Diary of a Writer* as a separate monthly publication that is entirely his own. *The Diary* quickly becomes popular and widely read.
1876–78	Continues publication of *The Diary*, which includes "The Golden Age in the Pocket" (1876), "The Boy at Christ's Christmas Tree" (1876), "The Peasant Marei" (1876), "A Gentle Creature" (1876), and "The Dream of a Ridiculous Man" (1877). In December 1877 Dostoevsky breaks off work on *The Diary* to start work on *The Brothers Karamazov*. His son Alexey dies unexpectedly at the age of three. Dostoevsky travels with Vladimir Solovyov to the Optina Pustyn Monastery and visits the famous Father Amvrosy, who comforts him with the words Father Zosima will use in *The Brother's Karamazov*. The unwritten *The Life of a Great Sinner* becomes an important source for this last novel.
1879	*The Brothers Karamazov* appears in the *Russian Herald* in numbers 1 and 2 (January–February). Subsequent installments appear regularly in numbers 4–6 (April–June), 8–11 (August–November), and in 1880, numbers 1, 4, and 7–11 (January, April, July–November). Readers treat the appearance of the novel as an important event.
1880	In June, delivers his famous "Pushkin Speech" at the celebration in Moscow in honor of the great poet. This event is Dostoevsky's last and greatest public triumph.
1881	On 28 January, suffering from chronic emphysema, dies from a hemorrhage of the lungs. On 1 February Dostoevsky is buried in the cemetery at the Aleksandr Nevsky Monastery.

It's terrible the things you find in those books.
—The mysterious visitor, in *The Brothers Karamazov*

Oh, those storytellers! They can't rest content with writing something useful, agreeable, palatable—they have to dig up all the
earth's most cherished secrets! . . . I'd forbid them to write, that's
what I'd do! I mean, have you ever known the like? A man reads . . .
and finds himself reflecting—and before he knows where he is, all
kinds of rubbish come into his head. I'd forbid them to write, truly I
would. I'd forbid them to write altogether!
—Epigraph to Dostoevsky's first published story, *Poor Folk*, drawn
from V. F. Odoevsky's "The Living Corpse" (1839).

Literary and Historical Context

1

Historical Context

In January 1879 readers of the conservative *Russian Herald* turned to the first installment of *The Brothers Karamazov* with excitement and intense expectation. The appearance of Fyodor Dostoevsky's newest and last novel was, quite simply, an event. Before undertaking a reading of *The Brothers Karamazov,* or for that matter, before reading any work of Russian literature, it is helpful for the Western reader to keep in mind that Russian literature is—and has traditionally been—taken very seriously by its audience. Why is this? Why is so much value placed on the word in the context of artistic discourse? The answer to this question is quite straightforward. Because of the intermittently repressive regimes of the Russian czars, the related arenas of literature and literary criticism have served as primary vehicles, particularly in the nineteenth century, for political, economic, and social discourse. That is, writers and thinkers often found that the safest way to express their ideas was indirectly—through the medium of literary art and discourse about that art.

In fact, by the 1860s the key debate about Russia—its future and its identity—was taking place through a complex dialogue between three of its greatest novelists—Ivan Turgenev, Leo Tolstoy, and Dostoevsky— and the so-called radical critics, Nikolai Chernyshevsky, Nikolai Dobroliubov, and Dmitri Pisarev, all followers of the first great Russian social critic, Vissarion Belinsky. Their debate often centered on the problem of the nature of art: should writers focus on the problems inherent to and arising from the work itself, or should art deliberately seek to serve socially utilitarian purposes? The first duty of art, argued the radical critics, is to serve the betterment of man; aesthetic considerations are secondary. Literature, they asserted, should depict reality in such a way that readers will be inspired to advocate fundamental social change, even revolution. No, argued the novelists, maintaining the aesthetic integrity of the literary text must remain the uppermost concern of the writer. Only then will the work genuinely serve the larger purposes of awakening the consciousnesses of its readers and creating in them a higher moral awareness.

Add to this general picture of the artist in nineteenth-century Russian society the ever-present censor. The most direct effect of censorship was to make the Russian writer resort to the techniques of Aesopian language more often than his counterparts in Europe or the United States found it necessary to do. Whether this resulted in better or worse writing is still a subject for debate. This situation was further muddied by the fact that one could not simply dismiss the censor as a villain, for the censor often had a double identity as writer. The example of Ivan Goncharov is a good case in point. Goncharov, the author of the magnificent and haunting novel *Oblomov* (1859), found himself in the difficult but not altogether unusual predicament of being both a liberal novelist and an official government censor charged with upholding an autocratic, restrictive regime.

The government censor was not the only censor with whom the Russian writer had to contend. Almost as insidious and difficult to coexist with from the 1860s onward was the subtle censorship shaped increasingly by the shared beliefs of the intellectual class, whose sympathies, according in part to the dictates of literary fashion, were becoming decidedly radical. This double bind, this dual censorship, has been eloquently described by Simon Karlinsky. He calls our attention to "the existence of two separate but equally repressive systems of censorship." The *de jure* censorship of the government had considerable power, but "far more powerful and, in the long run, even more oppressive was the *de facto* unofficial censorship by the anti-government literary critics, who not only ceaselessly demanded that all writers be topical, obviously relevant and socially critical, but also prescribed rigid formal and aesthetic criteria to which all literature was supposed to conform."[1] The great twentieth-century novelist Vladimir Nabokov has succinctly and aptly described the Russian writer's situation as a "strange double purgatory."[2]

What an irony it is then that the key distinguishing marks of the great Russian writers Aleksandr Pushkin, Mikhail Lermontov, Nikolai Gogol, Ivan Turgenev, Nikolai Leskov, Leo Tolstoy, Anton Chekhov, and, above all, Dostoevsky should exhibit precisely the opposite features. Despite the overriding differences among the visions of all these writers, they shared the conviction that literature need not, indeed, should not be narrowly topical. Most important, each author refused to conform to "rigid formal and aesthetic criteria"; instead, all of them were extraordinary innovators in artistic form. Thus, one way that we might begin to understand the historical context of Russian literature in the nineteenth century, and *The Brothers Karamazov* in particular, is that despite an unrelenting pressure from all sides on Dostoevsky and other writers, they consistently refused to conform to defined standards. Instead, they—and in particular, Dostoevsky—created a literature of extreme narrative inventiveness and mythic universality. *The Brothers Karamazov* stands as the greatest representative of this literature.

2

The Importance of The Brothers Karamazov

By using the phrase "greatest representative," I am taking a stand in an ongoing debate among critics about the nature and the validity of affirming that "great works" and a canon even exist. A book such as this one, an introductory volume that is part of a series, is in itself an affirmation of both ideas. Despite the widespread attack on the canon, I suspect that certain works, among them *The Brothers Karamazov*, will continue to be read, not because they subtly support the existence of certain reigning power structures but because of their aesthetic qualities, their passion, and the frisson of recognition they incite in their readers. *The Brothers Karamazov* exists as a happy blend of form and its transcendence. It has easily become a case study for widely varying literary theories and has prompted arguments about whether the meaning inherent in its pages opposes its author's actual intentions. The characters in this novel have attained the status of myth. Moreover, Dostoevsky, in this as in all his other novels, indirectly has encouraged his readers to duplicate in the act of reading the dilemmas of the characters. Dostoevsky's reader is an *implicated* reader.

From the outset of his literary career in 1846 Dostoevsky was a radical experimenter. He consistently sought new narrative forms and ceaselessly worked to portray "new types" of characters who had not yet been fictionally represented. Despite this continual reaching out to new forms and themes, however, Dostoevsky's created world has a curiously confined geography. Certain roads are traveled repeatedly from story to story and novel to novel, so that every inch of their terrain is charted in depth. Scandal scenes, confessions, inserted narratives, passionate, infernal women, grimy taverns, coffinlike rooms—these are the stock-in-trade of Dostoevsky's created world, yet this world, despite its familiar landmarks, remains provocative and uncontainable.

Each reader who enters this world discovers Dostoevsky's greatness anew and must, despite the successive generations that have preceded her as a reader, confront along the way the great and searching questions this writer asks us to contemplate. *The Brothers Karamazov* asks us to approach the problem of evil: How can one accept the suffering of children and still believe in a good and active God? Does a child have the right to raise his hand against the father who mistreats him? Who has the right to judge a criminal? How can one overcome the boundless grief felt at the loss of a beloved child? These are the kinds of questions that each reader of *The Brothers Karamazov* is asked to consider.

The last of these questions offered Dostoevsky the painful cornerstone of inspiration for this, his last and arguably greatest novel. Just as he was beginning work on the novel, Dostoevsky's youngest son, Alyosha, died at the age of three, apparently from an epileptic seizure. Inconsolable and nearly mad with grief, Dostoevsky, himself an epileptic, blamed himself for Alyosha's death because he believed the child had inherited his disease. Yet in the pages of *The Brothers Karamazov* Dostoevsky created through art the child he had lost and remade him as he might have become in Alyosha Karamazov. One cannot but think of Shakespeare, his lost son Hamnet, and his play *Hamlet*. Both works are, of course, intimately about the relations between fathers and their sons. Sigmund Freud, in his famous essay "Dostoevsky and Parricide" (1928), asserts that "*The Brothers Karamazov* is the most magnificent novel ever written: the episode of the Grand Inquisitor, one of the peaks in the literature of the world, can hardly be valued too highly. Before the problem of the creative artist, analysis must, alas, lay down its arms."[1]

Dostoevsky viewed his brand of fiction as "fantastic realism"— an oxymoronic term, certainly, but one worthy of our careful consideration. The following statement contains a kind of artistic credo: "I have my own special view of reality (in art), and what the majority call fantastic and exceptional sometimes constitutes the very essence of reality for me. In my opinion, the commonness of some occurrences and the conventional view of them are not realism at all, but even the contrary."[2]

Virginia Woolf was among the first Western readers to recognize this special quality of Dostoevsky's prose.

> Alone among writers Dostoevsky has the power of reconstructing those most swift and complicated states of mind. . . . This is the exact opposite of the method adopted, perforce, by most of our novelists. They reproduce all the external appearances—tricks of manner, landscape, dress, and the effect of the hero upon his friends—but very rarely, and only for an instant, penetrate to the tumult of thought which rages within his own mind. But the whole fabric of a book by Dostoevsky is made out of such material. . . . We have to get rid of the old tune which runs so persistently in our ears and to realize how little of our humanity is expressed in that old tune.[3]

Dostoevsky's life itself was characterized by just such a "tumult of thought" and by a kind of "fantastic realism." How many men find themselves, after a term of solitary imprisonment in a fortress, facing a virtually certain death by firing squad, only to be reprieved at the last moment by the arrival of a galloping messenger from the czar? Take into account, too, Dostoevsky's epilepsy, his years as a prisoner in a Siberian labor camp, his episodes of compulsive gambling, his affair with Polina Suslova while his first wife lay dying of consumption, and his probable belief that his father had been murdered by his own serfs. The stuff of Dostoevsky's life, as in the lives of so many Russian writers of the nineteenth century, was often far stranger, more violent, more fantastic, than the stuff of fiction.

3

Critical Reception

The critical reception of *The Brothers Karamazov* has been extraordinary and, whether positive or negative, intense. All of Dostoevsky's novels were published serially in the thick journals of the day, and each installment provoked discussion about both its literary qualities and its role in that great ongoing polemic about Russia and her future.

Toward the end of his life, as he was working on *The Brothers Karamazov*, Dostoevsky delivered his famous Pushkin speech. On 7 June 1880, on the night before his speech he wrote at midnight to his wife about the amazing reception he was receiving. Much of it he attributed to the positive critical reaction that *The Brothers Karamazov* had been attracting in each of its installments. "As I walked across the hall during intermission, a host of people, youths and graybeards and ladies, rushed toward me exclaiming, 'You're our prophet. We've become better people since we read *The Karamazovs*.' (In brief, I realized how tremendously important *The Karamazovs* is.)" The next evening, after the triumph of his speech, he wrote to her, "When I appeared on the stage, the auditorium thundered with applause. . . . I bowed and made signs, begging them to let me read—but to no avail: elation, enthusiasm (all because of *The Karamazovs*)!"[1]

In the years after Dostoevsky's death, some Russian critics and philosophers, such as Vladimir Solovyov and V. V. Rozanov, focused, almost as disciples, on Dostoevsky's religious ideas. Somewhat later, the Russian philosopher Nicholas Berdyaev concluded his book on Dostoevsky with the staggering assertion: "So great is the worth of Dostoevsky that to have produced him is by itself sufficient justification for the existence of the Russian people in the world; and he will bear witness for his countrymen in the last judgment of the nations."[2] Likewise, Dmitri Merezhkovsky regarded him as a great mystic. Far more critical was Nikolai Mikhailovsky, the radical populist, whose 1882 article "A Cruel Talent" depicts Dostoevsky as a sadist. Dostoevsky's own friend, the critic Nikolai Strakhov, contributed to this negative view of Dostoevsky by circulating after Dostoevsky's death the unfounded but unfortunately persistent rumor that Dostoevsky had once violated a young girl. Perhaps the best-known negative critics of Dostoevsky are Henry James, D. H. Lawrence, and, more recently, Vladimir Nabokov and Milan Kundera, although all four, on closer examination, are not nearly as derogatory about Dostoevsky's art as they have been described as being. For example, Lawrence complains, about *The Brothers Karamazov,* that he feels impatient with "these morbidly introspective Russians, morbidly wallowing in adoration of Jesus, then getting up and spitting in His beard. . . . It's all masturbation, half-baked, and one gets tired of it. One gets tired of being told that Dostoevsky's *Legend of the Grand Inquisitor* 'is the most profound declaration which ever was made about man and life.' . . . The more Dostoevsky gets worked up about the tragic nature of the human soul, the more I lose interest. I have read the Grand Inquisitor three times, and never can remember what it's really about." But then he also admits that he finds *The Brothers Karamazov* increasingly more depressing "because, alas, more drearily true to life. At first it had been lurid romance. Now I read *The Grand Inquisitor* once more, and my heart sinks right through my shoes."[3]

Dostoevsky began to be read widely outside of Russia during the 1880s. By 1912 Constance Garnett had undertaken her monumental project of translating Dostoevsky into English. By the twentieth century in the United States and Western Europe Dostoevsky had indeed become a major figure whose fictional style would be imitated by countless other writers and whose ideas would be appropriated by philosophers—especially the French existentialists, social thinkers, and students of psychology.

In the Soviet Union the reception to Dostoevsky has ebbed and flowed with the changing political climate, although virtually every decade of the twentieth century in Russia has managed, despite these political vagaries, to produce its great Dostoevsky scholars. Today Dostoevsky studies are literally flourishing. This is not the appropriate place for a survey of Dostoevsky criticism, but readers interested in such a survey would do well to turn to the works of Joseph Frank, Sergei Belov, G. M. Fridlender, William Leatherbarrow, Vladmir Seduro, and Victor Terras and to the helpful indexes published in the journal *Dostoevsky Studies*. Suffice it to say, the critical reaction to *The Brothers Karamazov* has continued unabated for over a hundred years. Each generation of readers discovers and remakes this novel anew. For those readers who are approaching this novel for the first time, I would urge you to gauge carefully the most important critical reception of all: your own. What follows is an introductory reading of the text with a modest goal: to enrich your response to this great work and to deepen your aesthetic pleasure in it.

A Reading

From Dostoevsky's notebook for the novel (1879). This page is from the notes for chapter 6 of Book V and has been reprinted in volume XV of the *Polnoe sobranie*. *The original manuscript is in Pushkinskii Dom in St. Petersburg.*

4

Of Prefaces, Preludes, and Parodies
PART I: BOOKS I, II, AND III

Dostoevsky, more than any other Russian novelist of the nineteenth century, tended in both his novels and his short stories to observe to some degree Aristotle's unities of time, place, and action. Part I of *The Brothers Karamazov* is no exception: its action encompasses a single day within the small, provincial fictional town of Skotoprigonevsk (in Russian this name signifies the place where cattle are herded together, or "cattlepen"). Yet these unities that Dostoevsky imposes in fact demarcate the opposite, for this single day teems with the memories and foreshadowings of other days, with events which have long since occurred or whose potential occurrence looms large, with philosophical dilemmas, with plots, with rage, and with humor.

Any reader beginning *The Brothers Karamazov* for the first time will discover that Part I lays out, often in comic form, the questions, the implied answers, and the sheer drama of the rest of the novel. The early events and each idea that the characters express at the beginning rhyme with other parts of the novel. Indeed, the very rhyming or interconnectedness of the parts of *The Brothers Karamazov* becomes the reader's own thread through the labyrinth of events and ideas that are to follow. This, then, is a novel of rhymes.[1] Characters, fragments of plot, fragments of time—all echo and reverberate in unexpected ways and places. An evil deed can find its parallel in a good one; the secret fantasies of one character can find an echo in the theories of another. A stray dog running through the back alleys can be an instrument of damnation or of salvation.

Perhaps nothing contributes more to the intensity of the interlocking rhymes in this novel than the epigraph. Dostoevsky gave epigraphs to only two of his major novels, *The Possessed* (1871) and *The Brothers Karamazov*. Both are from the Bible (although *The Possessed* has an epigraph from Pushkin as well as its epigraph from Luke 8:32–37). As with Tolstoy's *Anna Karenina* (1878), these biblical epigraphs offer up a kind of ground thesis to the novel; each author is also making a virtuoso showing of the immense variety of uses to which such an epigraph can be put.

Dostoevsky takes his epigraph from John 12:24: "Verily, verily, I say unto you, except a corn of wheat fall into the ground and die, it abideth alone: but if it die, it bringeth forth much fruit." *The Brothers Karamazov* is a novel that seeks to affirm the existence of miracle and to scrutinize its complexities, the uses to which it can be put, and its spontaneous, even gratuitous manifestations; it is a novel about salvation and damnation. The epigraph, in the many guises we see it assuming throughout the novel, becomes a kind of standard-bearer for these weighty, metaphysical themes, themes the modern reader tends to avoid.

But having asserted that this novel takes on such unresolvable matters of belief, such philosophical questions about the nature of evil, guilt, and love, let me hasten to assure the reader ready to balk that *The Brothers Karamazov* is by no means a dense religious tract or a dated, inaccessible, bulky thing. This novel has engrossed and moved numerous generations of readers. Although Dostoevsky may have had an appetite for exploring religious, philosophical, and moral questions, he did so as an artist who cared passionately about depicting the surface of character as well as its depth and who explored the innumerable ramifications of single, often simple acts.

By the time Dostoevsky began work on *The Brothers Karamazov*, he was financially secure and revered as one of Russia's greatest writers. He had been publishing the immensely successful *Diary of a Writer* (1873, 1876–81), which allowed him to reflect on society, politics, and history in a highly idiosyncratic form of his own—a blend of fact and fiction, or direct, hard-hitting journalistic polemic and indirect, subversively persuasive fiction. Yet Dostoevsky's novels contain, in different proportion, that same curious blend of fact with fiction, as does his most successful journalism, and *The Brothers Karamazov* proves to be no exception. Indeed, the opening paragraphs of the novel highlight Dostoevsky's strategic blending of the language of fact with that of fiction. He uses each in the service of the other.

Part I of *The Brothers Karamazov* contains three books, "The History of a Certain Family," "An Unfortunate Gathering," and "The Sensualists." Each of these titles reflects different narrative propensities of the figure whom Dostoevsky uses to get his story told—the narrator-chronicler. "The History of a Certain Family" alerts the reader immediately to the fact that the narrator-chronicler intends to proceed in an orderly fashion; his readers are to know something about the members of the Karamazov family before they actually encounter them—to use a favorite phrase of Dostoevsky in his notebooks—in a "field of action." "An Unfortunate Gathering" hints that the action of the novel will begin abruptly and scandalously—indeed, Dostoevsky and his many narrators have all had a penchant for scandal scenes. And finally, "The Sensualists" shows the reader that our narrator-chronicler, however fond he is of depicting "a certain family" or a particular "unfortunate gathering" also has a predilection for creating types, for discovering the generalization that lurks at the heart of the particular. One is reminded of the aphorism with which Tolstoy opens *Anna Karenina*: "All happy families resemble one another, but each unhappy family is unhappy in its own way." In that statement the general and the particular also coexist as categories of each other. All these hypotheses about the narrator-chronicler and his story, made simply by glancing at the table of contents of Dostoevsky's hefty novel, are, to some degree, borne out by a reading of Part I.

But, of course, these expectations are not fulfilled without some twists. There often exists a tension between the title of a book or chapter and its content—often, but not always. The "not always" is key: because the reader cannot predict what the narrator's stance will be, he or she cannot make judgments precipitously. The chapter title, "Peasant women who have faith," turns out to be sincere, but "A seminarian bent on a career" drips with irony and oxymoron. And what of the middle ground? What attitude does the narrator-chronicler imply by the three "Confession of an ardent heart" chapters, or by "The controversy"? Here irony and sympathetic sincerity intersect, and the reader must withhold judgment. Throughout this long novel, Dostoevsky uses his narrator-chronicler as a device to force us to make and remake judgments and, eventually, to learn when to suspend them.

Dostoevsky, in creating his peculiar narrator-chronicler—that voice which also narrates *The Idiot* (1868) and *The Possessed*—had found a vehicle by which, even as he practiced occasional deceptions, he could persuade the reader of his narrator's reliability. At the same time, the narrator-chronicler, by his fondness for making sociological and psychological pronouncements, by his irresistible desire to throw in hints of future events, and by his inability or even refusal to supply the facts of the matter at crucial moments, offered Dostoevsky a subtle means of manipulating his readers and making them duplicate indirectly some of the key experiences of his characters.

Yet behind this chatty, often digressive narrator lurks Dostoevsky, the conjurer who can convince us that all the actions and conversations in Books II and III took place in less than a single day. The action of Part I begins around 11:30 A.M. on a bright August day and ends sometime after nightfall. Dostoevsky, although he never wrote a play, was drawn to presenting vast chunks of his novels in sequential dramatic units. The scenes, linked for the most part by the movements of Alexey Fyodorovich Karamazov ("Alyosha"), take place in the monastery, in a back alley and garden, at Katerina Ivanovna's, and at a crossroads. The action begins and ends at the monastery, and along the way the humble settings of the small town take on a symbolic aura.

It is no wonder that Leonid Grossman, one of the major Russian critics of Dostoevsky, has called this novel a morality play.[2] Fyodor Karamazov highlights this morality-play quality by urging Alyosha to bring his pillow and mattress home from the monastery. Alyosha, as he moves back and forth from the monastery to his father's house, finds himself inhabiting a landscape that is as metaphoric as it is real. Two fathers—Fyodor Karamazov, his biological father, and Zosima, his spiritual father—compete for possession of his soul. He and his brothers undergo the trials typical of a protagonist in a morality play, so that the novel functions as a kind of polyphonic morality or mystery play. Yet even as we acknowledge the "morality play" atmosphere, we become immersed in the many realistic, often comic details with which the novel brims.

Chapter 1 is entitled "Fyodor Pavlovich Karamazov," yet the first words of the novel are "Alexey Fyodorovich Karamazov was the third son. . . ." Thus, the narrator-chronicler sets up an immediate tension over the focus of the ensuing paragraphs. Is Fyodor being described for his own merits or because he is the father of this future hero, Alyosha? As the reader moves through the novel, it becomes increasingly difficult to determine what is primary and what is variation, what is a main theme and what is a digression upon it.

Moreover, a novel that opens with a description of a third son who is in some ways a simpleton compared to his older brothers would seem to be a fairy tale. Before the reader has reached the second line of the novel, then, a series of conflicting expectations have been set up: we have moved from the epigraph from the Bible, to the apologetic, defensive, and chatty "From the Author," to the expository "History of a Certain Family," to the chapter title, "Fyodor Pavlovich Karamazov," to the fairy-tale beginning. The reader, by the time he or she arrives at the first sentence, has undergone a series of perspective jolts, a bumpy carriage ride indeed, to borrow a metaphor that will figure near the end of the novel. Our narrator-chronicler or our author seems to want to play it all ways at once.

The first paragraphs of the novel belie the fact that Part I of the novel will sound in a minor key the major themes of the novel. We learn in the first sentence that Fyodor Karamazov died "exactly thirteen years ago," which places the action in the 1860s. The closer one looks at the narrator's sociological and psychological description, the fuzzier its contours become. Old Karamazov is a "strange type, yet one pretty frequently to be met with," "senseless" yet "shrewd and intelligent." The narrator-chronicler evinces at the outset a strong propensity to qualify and elaborate each statement he makes, yet his qualifications serve to confuse rather than to clarify. A smokescreen of words emerges, yet through them we gradually begin, by the sheer accumulation of detail and description, to understand the qualities of the buffoon Fyodor Karamazov.

Russian readers of the nineteenth century would have tended to identify this chatty, slightly absurd prose style with the work of Nikolai Gogol. Dostoevsky was indeed deeply influenced by Gogol, particularly by his narrative style in which generalizations are frequently illustrated with examples that muddle rather than explicate. We read of Karamazov's first bizarre marriage to Adelaida Ivanovna, the mother of the oldest son, Dmitri. Her marriage to Fyodor, we learn, was an absurd echo of "foreign ideas, and was also due to the irritation caused by lack of mental freedom" (*BK*, 5). When "Mitya" was three, Adelaida Ivanovna ran off with a poor divinity student, and later, when Fyodor learns of her death, two stories about his reaction circulate: the first, that he ran into the street and shouted for joy; the second, that he "wept without restraint like a little child." By this point the reader has been assaulted by a mass of comic and contradictory detail. Fyodor himself seems more like caricature than character. Yet lest we fall into too comfortable a distance from the narrative, the narrator-chronicler, by a deft refocusing of perspective, suddenly draws us into the action. The chapter ends: "It is quite possible that both versions were true, that he rejoiced at his release, and at the same time wept for her who released him. As a general rule, people, even the wicked, are much more naive and simple-hearted than we suppose. And we ourselves are too" (*BK*, 4). The boundaries have shifted abruptly. We are forced momentarily into an uncomfortable identification with the repulsive Fyodor Pavlovich, at whom we may have just been smiling. Such shifts occur throughout the novel. Chapter 1 offers a paradigm of how suddenly these changes of focus can be effected.

Throughout the course of Part I, Dostoevsky and his narrator-chronicler offer a kind of smorgasbord of the narrative devices and, more important, the themes that will figure most prominently in the novel. Under the guise of introducing Zosima and the Karamazov family, the narrator-chronicler puts in motion a complicated plot involving money, insult, sexual rivalries between brothers and between father and son, and the expectation of crime.

The opening situation of the novel is a peculiar one: a biological family assembles for the first time in many years in its hometown, from which all the members have been absent for a prolonged period. "Some of its members met for the first time in their lives" (*BK*, 12). Even Fyodor Karamazov and his reputed bastard son Smerdyakov have recently been away from Skotoprigonevsk. Their gathering becomes for the characters, as well as for the narrator and the reader, an occasion both for intimacy, often angry intimacy, and for explanations and stories about the past. As the three Karamazov brothers—Dmitri (who is 27), Ivan (24), and Alyosha (20)—get acquainted, they tell each other their stories. Thus Dostoevsky introduces important plot material through dramatic dialogue and confessional monologue rather than through a more distanced third-person narrative of events.

As an artist, Dostoevsky sought, whenever possible, to render events through the prism of first-person narrative. As the novel progresses, we see precisely how important it was to him that characters express their ideas in their own way. Although Dostoevsky tends to be regarded as the novelist of ideas par excellence, we must not forget that for him the depiction of character was equally important. Ideas were exciting and meaningful in their representation through particular characters. So, for example, the idea of "active love" as expressed by Zosima and by Dmitri are two very different things.

MEMORY AND FORGETTING

The themes of memory and forgetting, so crucial to the novel as a whole, find their first expression in the often mindless actions of Fyodor Karamazov. We learn that, after the death of his first wife, he "completely abandoned" Dmitri, "not from malice, nor because of his matrimonial grievances, but simply because he forgot him." Upon the death of Fyodor's second wife, Sofya Ivanovna—the mother of Ivan and Alyosha—"almost exactly the same thing happened to the two little boys as to their elder brother, Mitya. They were completely forgotten and abandoned by their father" (*BK*, 5, 8).

Counterposed to Fyodor's monstrous acts of forgetfulness are Alyosha's indelible memories of his mother. Although he was orphaned at four years, "strange as it seems, I know that he remembered his mother all his life, like a dream, of course" (*BK*, 8). In fact, his most precious memory of her provides a rich core of meaning that reverberates and resurfaces in other ways throughout the novel. I quote the account in its entirety because each element will refract and travel through the novel:

> I have mentioned already, by the way, that though he lost his mother in his fourth year, he remembered her all his life—her face, her caresses, "as though she stood living before me." Such memories may persist, as everyone knows, from an even earlier age, even from two years old, but scarcely standing out through a whole lifetime like spots of light out of darkness, like a corner torn out of a huge picture, which was all faded and disappeared except that fragment. That is how it was with him. He remembered one still summer evening, an open window, the slanting rays of the setting sun (he recalled the slanting rays most vividly of all); in a corner of the room the holy image, before it a lighted lamp, and on her knees before the image his mother, sobbing hysterically with cries and shrieks, snatching him up in both arms, squeezing him close till it hurt, and praying for him to the mother of God . . . holding him out in both arms to the image as though to put him under the mother's protection . . . and suddenly a nurse runs in and snatches him from

her in terror. That was the picture! And Alyosha remembered his mother's face at that minute. (*BK*, 13)

Thus in these early chapters a vital tension operates between forgetting and remembering. This tension will gain a talismanlike force as the novel progresses. Moreover, the passage above contains numerous strands that, as Robert Belknap was the first to point out, tend to reappear whenever Dostoevsky sounds one of his primary themes: the working out of divine grace in the world.[3]

POLYPHONY

Each generation of critics has rediscovered the profoundly musical tonality of Dostoevsky's fiction, particularly of his big novels. In the late 1920s Mikhail Bakhtin described Dostoevsky's novels as polyphonic, and *The Brothers Karamazov* as the polyphonic novel par excellence: "*A plurality of independent and unmerged voices and consciousnesses, a genuine polyphony of fully valid voices is in fact the chief characteristic of Dostoevsky's novels* [Bakhtin's italics]." But Bakhtin also identifies certain limits to the scope of this polyphony. The endings of the novels and, ultimately, the role of the author as a conductor or orchestrator of the many other voices both somewhat contain this powerful polyphonic impulse. "We will say that almost all of Dostoevsky's novels have a *conventionally literary,* conventionally monologic ending. . . . In essence only *The Brothers Karamazov* has a completely polyphonic ending [Bakhtin's italics]." Much later, in his notes of 1961, Bakhtin clarifies his view of Dostoevsky's role as author of the polyphonic novel. "Our point of view in no way assumes a passivity on the part of the author. . . . The author is profoundly *active,* but his activity is of a special *dialogic* sort. . . . Dostoevsky frequently interrupts, but never drowns out the other's voice [Bakhtin's italics]."[4] Moreover, this polyphony operates simultaneously at different levels—in the interplay among characters, within a single character, among fragments of the plot, and, most important, through the many kinds of narrative in the novel. Thus readers must be able to listen—if they are to experience the text as a whole—not to a single "spokesman" but to several "voices" within the same sentence: the narrator, the character, and perhaps a character whose voice is being parodied or quoted.

The passage in which the narrator-chronicler describes Alyosha's precious memory of his mother exemplifies one of the many ways in which the overarching polyphony of the novel works. Imagine the rotation of a kaleidoscope in which identical shapes rearrange themselves into new patterns, which set up in the observer's mind varying responses, varieties of connotation. Persisting memories from childhood, spots of light amid darkness, a still summer evening, an open window, the slanting rays of the setting sun, a holy icon, a lighted lamp, a parent's tears, a picture created through memory—each of these elements somehow, according to Dostoevsky's private mythology, contributes intimately and directly to an ever-shifting yet unified design that reflects the epiphanic moments of grace that can occur unexpectedly in human life.

Dostoevsky reworks these elements throughout the course of the novel; they recombine in new ways. This intense reworking into new combinations of a finite set of different components constitutes an organized polyphony of poetics. Moreover, this particular form of expression meshes, as is frequently the case in Dostoevsky's fiction, with the particular idea he is seeking to express. Form and content become inseparable. Dostoevsky's idea here, to put it in its simplest terms, is that a precious memory of love can exert a unique, sustaining, and unexpected power over people. As the reader continues through the novel, these often repeated verbal fragments, associated with important moments in the lives of the characters, begin to figure in the structure of the novel. They work upon the reader in the same way in which they have worked upon Alyosha—as spots of light in the darkness.

Other themes sounded in Part I work themselves out in similar fashion—the expectation of a miracle, the desire to confess and to practice confession, the right of one person to judge and forgive another, the practice of using reason to challenge religious belief, the sense that a crime will occur, the testing of the bonds that exist among members of a family. Each of these themes has a positive and a negative dimension; all present themselves to the reader in a state of tension—all, to use a phrase to which the narrator and several of the characters are partial, cut both ways.

ALYOSHA

The narrator-chronicler chooses to describe the third son, "the hero" Alyosha, first. He has already stressed in his preface that Alyosha is by no means a great man. In fact, in Part I the narrator-chronicler characterizes him as almost a *yurodivyi,* "religious eccentric." In Russian this word has special connotations. Within the Russian Orthodox tradition a *yurodivyi,* or "God's fool," was a figure of either genuine or feigned foolishness who was believed to have the gift of prophecy.

Dostoevsky had long been fascinated with the figure of the *yurodivyi.* Prince Myshkin, the main character of *The Idiot,* exhibits many of the characteristics of this figure. While working on this novel, Dostoevsky had the idea of portraying a positively good man, a kind of Christ figure come to contemporary Russia. He set himself the artistic problem—drawing directly from Cervantes' Don Quixote, Dickens's Pickwick, and Hugo's Jean Valjean—of making goodness, which he knew was often inherently dull to read about, interesting. Dostoevsky felt that in many ways *The Idiot* was a failure and that in it he had not expressed "even a tenth" of what he had wanted to. Nevertheless, he always maintained a special fondness for this novel.

Hence it is of interest that in the early notes for *The Brothers Karamazov* Alyosha is described as "the idiot." This suggests that Dostoevsky hoped to rework, with greater success, the character of the good man. So while the narrator-chronicler describes Alyosha as being "almost" a *yurodivyi,* he is also quick to endow the young man with health, strength, and handsomeness. But Alyosha does retain certain qualities that make him different from others: he inspires love wherever he goes; he exhibits a "wild fanatical modesty and chastity"; he does not resent insults, although "no one looked on him as a simpleton or naive person." This observation clashes with the narrator's earlier assertion that he was almost a *yurodivyi.* The reader must eventually sort out the seeming contradiction. Finally, the narrator-chronicler observes, "there was something about him which made one feel at once (and it was so all his life afterwards) that he did not care to be a judge of others, that he would never take it upon himself to censure and would never condemn anyone for anything" (*BK,* 13). As such, Alyosha is the perfect repository for the confessions of his brothers and would seem to have the makings of an ideal future "elder."

As Miusov, Mitya's relative and former joint guardian, says, "Here is perhaps the one man in the world whom you might leave alone without a penny, in the center of a strange city of a million inhabitants, and he would not come to harm, he would not die of cold and hunger, for he would be fed and sheltered at once, and if he were not, he would find a shelter for himself, and it would cost him no effort or humiliation, and to shelter him would be no burden, but on the contrary, would probably be looked on as a pleasure" (*BK*, 15). Miusov's aphoristic and pithy characterization of Alyosha reflects some of the main action of Part I, for there is a virtual contest over who will give him shelter. Moreover, by the end of Part I several characters have declared their love for him; he is loved with many different kinds of love, all of which he accepts. Alyosha's wanderings around the town give us the structural framework of the novel: throughout Part I he functions as a kind of Jamesian *ficelle* (thread) who ties the action together by delivering and receiving notes and messages from other characters and who, above all, listens to their confessions.

It is typical of Dostoevsky that he should give the voicing of such an apt formulation of Alyosha's character to the slightly ridiculous Miusov, a liberal of the 1840s from whose views Dostoevsky would have been at pains to separate himself. Yet Dostoevsky frequently places his canniest formulations and even some of his most precious ideas into the mouths of characters who are for the most part negative. His inclination to do this contributes greatly to the polyphony and to the multivoicedness that Bakhtin has observed in his work and alerts the reader that she would do well to pay attention to virtually any character who appears, however briefly.

Alyosha returns to Skotoprigonevsk to see his mother's grave. The narrator gives us this important information, then waffles about it. "He practically acknowledged at the time that that was the only object of his visit. But it can hardly have been the whole reason of it. It is more probable that he himself did not understand and could not explain what had suddenly arisen in his soul, and drawn him irresistibly into a new, unknown, but inevitable path." Alyosha is drawn to his mother's grave by the force of a precious memory, yet, predictably, Fyodor Pavlovich could not show him the grave for he had "entirely forgotten where she was buried" (*BK*, 16).

Dostoevsky built countless structural harmonics into his novel, and one of them stems from this haphazardly and quickly reported scene. For when we last see Alyosha in the novel it will be at another memorial stone; there will be present another buffoonish father—one who embodies the power of memory as strongly as Fyodor exemplifies forgetfulness. It is the servant Grigory, another father figure in this novel, which has so many potential and actual fathers, who finally takes Alyosha to his mother's grave. Alyosha stands there with bowed head, until he walks away "without uttering a word" (*BK*, 17). Again, the situation rhymes, this time through contrast, with the scene at the end of the novel, where Alyosha will have some words to speak.

Alyosha's desire to see his mother's grave sets up a positive, yet absurdly unexpected response in Fyodor. He pays the monastery 1,000 rubles for requiems for the soul of his wife—yet not Alyosha's mother, but his first wife, the one who "used to thrash him" (*BK,* 17). Dostoevsky here comically parodies his own serious thoughts about causality and expectation, about the unpredictable and mysterious way in which one is influenced by the emotions or deeds of another. It is also Fyodor who first ludicrously suggests two key functions that Alyosha, as a future monk, might perform specifically for him and, by extension, for others—prayer, and spreading God's truth. "And do you know, I'm sorry to lose you, Alyosha; would you believe it, I've really grown fond of you. Well, it's a good opportunity. You'll pray for us sinners; we have sinned too much here. I've always been thinking who would pray for me, and whether there's anyone in the world to do it." He then urges Alyosha off to the monastery, "but go and get at the truth there, and then come and tell me." Fyodor concludes with a prediction that resembles those of Alyosha's spiritual father, Zosima, as well as that of the narrator-chronicler in his preface. "You will burn and you will burn out; you will be healed and come back again" (*BK,* 18, 19).

Yet Dostoevsky takes pains in Part I to remove Alyosha from the rigid role of being simply an emblem of goodness and potential godliness. Through his narrator-chronicler, through the words of other characters, and through Alyosha's own gently experienced doubts, Dostoevsky tries to depict, however tentatively, a darker side to Alyosha's character and to suggest his capacity, like any other human being, to slip into grave error. The narrator quickly points out to us that, although Alyosha is a believer, he is also "more of a realist than anyone." This distinction is key to the theological underpinnings of the novel, for Alyosha's faith has not been purchased through miracle. "Faith does not, in the realist, spring from the miracle, but the miracle from faith" (*BK,* 20). Dostoevsky, through his narrator-chronicler, here puts forth a concept of belief that is close to William James's doctrine of the "will to believe." The narrator-chronicler takes the example of the Apostle Thomas, who said that he would not believe until he saw. "Was it the miracle forced him to believe?" he asks. And answers, "Most likely not, but he believed solely because he desired to believe." Thus, in a passing example, the narrator-chronicler asserts that the most authentic religious belief arises from a desire to believe, a desire or will that is far more fundamental than any miracle. Miracles, for the sincere believer, confirm rather than purchase faith. Nevertheless, the realist and believing Alyosha expects a miracle to occur at the death of Zosima, and this expectation is dangerous. "The conviction that after his death the elder would bring extraordinary glory to the monastery was even stronger in Alyosha than in anyone else" (*BK*, 24).

Alyosha, in his first dialogue with the seminarian Rakitin, admits that he too has imagined that a terrible crime might take place between his father and his brothers. The sly and cynical Rakitin welds together these two omnipresent expectations—of a miracle and of a crime—by asserting that Zosima, "the old man," has with his "keen nose sniffed a crime. Your house stinks of it." He suggests that Zosima's bow to Mitya is a prophecy of this crime, and that Zosima hopes his prophecy will be remembered "to his glory." Rakitin also makes an accusation that will be repeated later in one of the most important moments of the novel: he finds Alyosha guilty of plagiarism—"You're quoting your elder's phrases" (*BK*, 68, 69, 72). Yet if *The Brothers Karamazov* is about the way in which grace travels through the world, what does plagiarism mean in this context?[5] Is not Alyosha already, at this early moment in the novel, doing precisely what his buffoonish father had jestingly predicted he would?

In Book III Dmitri begins his confession to Alyosha and calls him "an angel" (*BK*, 93). Yet the scene with Rakitin in which Alyosha admits that he well understands the Karamazov mentality has prepared us for Alyosha's identification with his swashbuckling brother. In fact, although Dmitri does not know it, Alyosha here commits a second act of plagiarism. Earlier that day Rakitin had said, "You are pure, but you've been down into the depths. . . . You're a Karamazov yourself; you're a thorough Karamazov—no doubt birth and selection have something to answer for. You're a sensualist from your father, a crazy saint from your mother" (*BK*, 70). Thus, when Dmitri describes his own "insect lust," Alyosha's comforting reply has assimilated and transformed Rakitin's taunt: "I am the same as you are. . . . The ladder's the same. I'm at the bottom step, and you're above, somewhere about the thirteenth. . . . But it's all the same. Absolutely the same in kind. Anyone on the bottom step is bound to go up to the top one" (*BK*, 98). Even though Dmitri tells Alyosha he is "going too far" in affirming the similarity between them, Mitya has himself, in an excess of emotion a few moments earlier, proclaimed the same truth: "All we Karamazovs are such insects, and angel as you are, that insect lives in you, too, and will stir up a tempest in your blood" (*BK*, 96). Thus, by the end of Part I, when Alyosha finally returns to the monastery to sleep, we have seen him, in one short day, loved as an angel and chosen as the interlocutor for confessions. Yet he has also been characterized as a *yurodivyi* and described as having the same potential for sensuality as his unruly brothers. Such is our "saintly" hero.

DMITRI

Although the narrator-chronicler proclaims Alyosha to be the hero, the drama of Part I revolves around Dmitri, whose arrival at the family meeting with Zosima the other characters are eagerly, often angrily, expecting. The first thing he does on entering the room is to make a low bow to Zosima. By the end of Part I it is evident that the act of bowing has evolved from a relatively perfunctory social act to a full-fledged symbol of the complexities of Dmitri's nature and the dilemmas of his moral situation. Since Dmitri yearns, above all, to be a man of honor, the bow is an apt gesture to attain symbolic status with regard to him. As we shall quickly see, such symbols adhere readily to Mitya; by the close of Part I back alleys, sums of money, and even a sword will all have become symbols expressive of his potential.

Dostoevsky deploys varied strategies to bring his characters to life. Alyosha takes shape from the narrator-chronicler's descriptions and as other characters tell him their ideas and their troubles. He often remains silent or borrows the words of others, makes them his own, then transmits them to someone else. It is the narrator-chronicler who gives most of the background information about Alyosha—even Alyosha's private memory of his mother comes from the narrator's perspective.

Yet the narrator-chronicler gives us only perfunctory descriptions of Mitya. Instead, it is through dialogue, through the words of others, and especially through his own words, that he springs to life. Fyodor's screeching harangue in the chapter "Why is such a man alive?" offers one view of Mitya's personality, as well as some vital plot information. It is Fyodor who first tells, though in skewed form, of the relationship between Katerina Ivanovna and Mitya and of the dreadful, dangerously incestuous triangles existing between Mitya, Fyodor, and Grushenka and between Ivan, Mitya, and Katerina Ivanovna. Moreover, Fyodor applies a kind of sexual imagery to describe this situation that strongly resembles the way in which Mitya will later talk about himself. These two sensualists are initially the only two who recognize that Grushenka, the supposedly loose woman, is virtuous. Fyodor observes, "Dmitri Fyodorovich wants to open this fortress with a golden key" (*BK*, 62). His metaphor neatly identifies Mitya's sexual energy with his desperate desire for money, while at the same time managing to suggest Grushenka's virtue.

It is also Fyodor who makes the first allusion to what will develop into the major subplot of the novel: he relates that Mitya got into an argument with his father's agent, Captain Snegiryov, in a tavern, seized him by the beard, and publicly insulted him. Dmitri's involvement in what subsequently becomes the story of Ilyusha and his family is thus foreshadowed, as is Dmitri's ready admission of guilt and repentance: "I behaved like a brute to that captain, and I regret it now, and I am disgusted with myself for it." Through this anecdote, we see Mitya as a man capable of both thoughtless, passionate violence and an equally quick repentance for it. Moreover, Mitya's response to Fyodor's diatribe brings out what will prove to be a critical theme for Mitya: the tension-fraught and often hazy boundary between a lie and the truth. "It's all a lie! Outwardly it's the truth, but inwardly, a lie!" (*BK*, 63).

Yet even as Mitya regrets his brutal rage toward his father's agent, he collapses into another fury, one directed at its true source—his father, not his father's surrogate or proxy. "Why is such a man alive?" he growls. Fyodor's reply at last brings to the surface what has been simmering beneath it all along: "Listen, listen, monks, to the parricide" (*BK*, 65).

In the early sections of his notes for the novel, Dostoevsky named the character who became Mitya, Ilyinsky. The genesis of his character is particularly interesting because, as Victor Terras points out, of the three brothers, "only Dmitri is a truly new type: Ivan and Alyosha have their predecessors . . . and versions of them existed in Dostoevsky's mind long before he started his last novel."[6]

However new an artistic creation he may have been, Mitya has both a direct literary and an actual genealogy. A Russian reader would see in Mitya's early biography a strong resemblance to other romantic heroes of nineteenth-century Russian fiction, particularly Pechorin in Lermontov's *A Hero of Our Time* (1840). His flaunted attractiveness to women, his recklessness, his attitude toward money, his stint in the Caucasus—these qualities and experiences are earmarks of the Russian romantic hero.

Dostoevsky's real-life source for Mitya came from a vastly different realm—his own experience as a prisoner in Siberia over 30 years earlier. Ilyinsky was a fellow prisoner who was serving out a 20-year sentence for parricide. Dostoevsky had written about him, though not by name, in his fictionalized prison memoir, *Notes from the House of the Dead* (1861).

> He was a nobleman, had served [in the army], and was something like a prodigal son to his sixty-year-old father. He was completely dissolute in character and had run heavily into debt. His father tried to restrain him, to bring him to his senses. But the father had a house and a farm, was thought to have money, and the son killed him, eager to get his inheritance. . . . He did not confess. He was deprived of his nobility and rank and sent to hard labor for twenty years. During the entire period I lived with him he was in the best and happiest frame of mind. He was flighty, thoughtless, irresponsible to an extraordinary degree, but he was no fool. . . . Of course I did not believe in that crime. But people from his town who knew all the details of his story told me all about his case. The facts were so clear that it was impossible to doubt them.[7]

Thus, although Mitya is a new creation for Dostoevsky, he is an amalgam of recognizable, though widely disparate, sources drawn from fiction as well as fact.

In Book III, "The Sensualists," the landscape and landmarks of Skotoprigonevsk take on a markedly metaphysical hue. When Alyosha, on his way to Katerina Ivanovna's, takes a "shortcut" through the back alleys and meets Mitya, their meeting is obviously charged from the outset with symbolic overtones. These same back alleys have already dominated the first two chapters of Book III as the locale for both the rape, years before, of "Stinking Lizaveta" and for her subsequent delivery of Smerdyakov. As Alyosha hurries along a "short cut by the back way," he wishes, without hope, that he could see Dmitri before the "fateful interview" with Katerina Ivanovna. His sudden meeting with Dmitri is as unexpected as it is welcome. In this "deserted garden" Dmitri launches into his three-part confession to Alyosha (*BK*, 91, 92).

Of Prefaces, Preludes, and Parodies

It is a commonplace to discover in the three Karamazov brothers an allegory about spirit (Alyosha), mind (Ivan), and body or heart (Mitya). But this classification becomes woefully inadequate and thin once one takes more than a cursory glance at them. Mitya's confession to Alyosha offers a dynamic case in point. At the outset of Mitya's confession, we discover that he is undergoing spiritual torment as well as 'the more expected agonies of love. His confession also sets up a paradigm for action in the novel. Just as in chapter 3 of Book II the peasant women came to Zosima to confess, so here Alyosha, beginning already to follow in the footsteps of his elder, receives the confessions of his brother.

Mitya's confession, as Belknap has pointed out, likewise shows his considerable skill as a narrator and demonstrates, extremely aptly, that he is a character of numerous potentials—a character poised on the brink, where any of several modes of action are equally possible (Belknap, 25–26, 72–73). Dmitri adroitly portrays himself; at the same time Dostoevsky maneuvers behind him, laying the groundwork for his mystery-thriller. Readers are asked to read this novel as they would a nineteenth-century "penny dreadful" or a twentieth-century murder mystery: they must sift and sort and watch for clues to a dreadful, impending action that has not yet occurred. Dostoevsky habitually casts his readers into several roles at once. They must be avidly devoted to following a plot, interested in philosophical and religious questions, and willing, like the readers of the modern novel, to stand apart from the narrator and make their own sense of the fictional world before them.

Dmitri shrewdly prefaces his own achingly personal confession with a literary preamble in which he quotes many of Dostoevsky's favorite writers, most notably, the nineteenth-century Russian poet Nikolai Nekrasov and the German writer Friedrich Schiller. The brothers sit together in a gazebo in "the most secluded corner" of a "deserted garden," and the word *secret* dominates the chapter. " 'Why do I whisper? Devil take it!' cried Dmitri Fyodorovich at the top of his voice. 'You see what silly tricks nature plays on one. I am here in secret, and I am guarding a secret. I'll explain later on, but knowing it's a secret, I began to speak secretly and to whisper like a fool, when there's no need' " (*BK*, 92).

Mitya has, even in his agitation, the sense that he is a narrator with a good story to tell. "I will explain everything, as they say, 'the story will be continued.' . . . Have you ever felt, have you ever dreamt of falling down a precipice into a pit? That's just how I'm falling, but not in a dream" (*BK*, 93). Mitya here echoes the rhythms of the epigraph: his sense of plunging into the pit evokes the dying of the seed.

But even as he invokes the precipice, he is, like any good author, acutely aware of the happy coincidence between the setting for his confession and that which he is about to confess. If we as readers have become faintly aware that the back alleys and deserted gardens have taken on a whiff of the symbolic, Mitya is one step ahead of us. "And you were going by the back way! Oh gods, I thank you for sending him by the back way." Just as Fyodor Pavlovich had earlier heralded Alyosha's role in the novel comically, Mitya states it seriously: "You are an angel on earth. You will hear and judge and forgive" (*BK*, 94).

Throughout his career, Dostoevsky was both attracted and repelled by the act of confession—attracted by its moments of rare and precious authenticity, repelled by the many self-justificatory and arrogant uses to which it could be put. Indeed, virtually every work of fiction Dostoevsky wrote contains some grain of his fascination with the act of confession. In *The Brothers Karamazov* the reader can discern a compendium of Dostoevsky's many responses to the confessional act. Early on the narrator-chronicler describes the custom of constant confession to a holy elder. He also cites the keen criticisms that had been leveled against this practice. Here Mitya's lengthy literary preface to his own confession is impressive yet risky, for it may suggest a Stavrogin-like arrogance (*The Possessed*) that could undermine its sincerity. Yet Mitya himself is sharply aware of the dangers of what he is attempting, "if only I'm not lying. I pray God I'm not lying now and showing off" (*BK*, 95).

Dmitri begins with a deliberate effort to create an atmosphere of secrecy. He ends the first part of his confession with a spiritual declaration of his understanding of the human condition that also invokes the idea of a secret—"everything in the world is a riddle" (*BK*, 96). This frequently quoted passage gives evidence of one of those tangled skeins where meaning overlaps meaning, and Mitya's words will eventually take on a poetic resonance, with uncanny reverberations throughout the novel.

Indeed, one could offer up a reading of *The Brothers Karamazov* that only focuses on such significant nodules in the text: Ivan's recitation to Alyosha of his "poem" of the Grand Inquisitor, Alyosha's response, Grushenka's story of the onion, Zosima's autobiography as told to Alyosha, Alyosha's vision of Cana of Galilee, and Alyosha's words to the boys at the end of the novel. Notice, too, that these events share certain features: Alyosha is always present; in each incident a story is told—that is, the narrated event is somehow separated from the mediated flow of the narrator-chronicler's voice; and in each incident words are important—the effect of one person's words upon another. The seeds of the epigraph find another manifestation as words in the novel.

Mitya expresses a desire that subsequently becomes primary for Ivan and Alyosha, as well as Zosima: he wishes to cling forever to Mother Earth but does not know how to. (Dostoevsky was one of the founders of the *pochvennichestvo* movement. Thus, when his characters express the desire to kiss the earth and water it with their tears, they are echoing a fundamental belief of their creator.)[8] Mitya closes the first part of his confession with a poetic recapitulation of its major themes. The atmosphere of secrecy with which he began now deepens into a metaphysical and Manichaean statement:

> Beauty! I can't endure the thought that a man of lofty mind and heart begins with the ideal of the Madonna and ends with the ideal of Sodom. What's still more awful is that a man with the ideal of Sodom in his soul does not renounce the ideal of the Madonna, and his heart may be on fire with that ideal, genuinely on fire, just as in his days of youth and innocence. Yes, man is broad, too broad, indeed. I'd have him narrower. The devil only knows what to make of it! What to the mind is shameful is beauty and nothing else to the heart. Is there beauty in Sodom? Believe me, that for the immense mass of mankind beauty is found in Sodom. Did you know that secret? God and the devil are fighting there and the battlefield is the heart of man. (*BK*, 97)

The pit into which he falls will become the unlikely locale for his redemption. "For when I do leap into the abyss, I go headlong with my heels up, and am pleased to be falling in that degrading attitude, and consider it something beautiful. And in the very depths of that degradation I begin a hymn of praise" (*BK*, 96). Mitya's flowery phrases foreshadow precisely what he will later do.

What is the effect of having Mitya's artistic, spiritual, veiled confession precede his more substantive one? Do his general observations about the human condition make us less shocked by what follows and more disposed to justify his behavior? At the beginning of the second part of his confession—in "anecdote"—Mitya embellishes on the back alley motif: locale modulates into moral location. "But I always like side paths, little dark back alleys behind the main road—there one finds adventures and surprises and precious metal in the dirt." Once again, Mitya the artist leaves the reader little room to make his or her own analysis. "I am speaking figuratively, brother. In the town I was in, there were no such back alleys in the literal sense, but morally there were" (*BK*, 97). What is left for readers to do when the character makes what seem to be the very associations they themselves would like to make? We are cast aside from analysis; instead, we simply become witnesses of a struggle. Yet perhaps the simple matter of bearing witness will become crucial for character and reader alike.

Moreover, the reader must begin to differentiate between the effects that the same truth has coming from the mouths of different characters. In Book II the unsavory Rakitin had called Alyosha a "thorough Karamazov" and "a sensualist." Now Mitya, whom we are predisposed to like and trust, is telling Alyosha the same thing, and Alyosha, as we have seen, agrees with him. This cluster of repetitions, of ideas and words that travel in a complex course of their own, regardless of who voices them, contributes to the "fantastic realism" of the novel and to the sense the reader has of entering a fully embodied world. Later, these verbal chains become more complex: the ideas of Ivan and Zosima, for example, find expression in characters who have never met either of these men; words become mediated and remediated—they float and settle like gossamer on the wind, like spores, or seeds. These words and ideas take on different aspects depending on who utters them.

At last Mitya begins to tell Alyosha his own story. We have already read descriptions of Mitya by the narrator and by other characters. Now the narratively astute Mitya describes himself. He has already given his view of the human condition; now we glimpse his own. He recalls that, as a lieutenant in a small town, he had managed to learn that his colonel, Katerina Ivanovna's father, had appropriated 4,500 rubles of government money. His account reads like a short story; like a short story, its artistic success depends on the narrator's ability to telescope the complexities and potentials of a character's whole life into a single incident. Mitya achieves this by keeping his promise to tell Alyosha "the whole truth just as it happened" (*BK*, 102).

We witness at firsthand the struggle between God and the devil in Mitya's heart. Mitya crisply presents that amorphous conflict in terms of three potential scenarios that occur to him during his moment of crisis. Katerina Ivanovna comes to his room, ready to offer herself in exchange for the 4,500 rubles which he had hinted to Katerina's half-sister Agatha he might be willing to give Katerina if she would come to him "secretly" (*BK*, 101). Mitya reveals that his "first idea was a—Karamazov one." He nearly swoons with the desire to possess her on the spot, although he knows that he would go to her with a proposal of marriage the next day. "It seemed as if there could be no resisting it; as though I should act like a bug, like a venomous spider, without a spark of pity" (*BK*, 102). But even as he contemplates this option, he realizes that she would, that next day, spurn him. This realization awakens both his spite and his second plan for action. The Karamazov idea modulates into the tradesman's idea: he imagines spurning her, and saying carelessly and contemptuously: "Two hundred if you like, with all my heart. But four thousand is not a sum to throw away on such frivolity" (*BK*, 103). Sensuality governs this idea as profoundly as it does the first, for Mitya realizes that the ecstasy of that moment of delicious "infernal revenge" would be worth a lifetime of regret.

But the third scenario, the course of action that Mitya actually takes, comes upon us suddenly. Mitya describes it purely dramatically; he offers no motivation or explanation, simply the most penetrating and riveting description. Likewise at other crucial moments of action throughout the novel motivations and explanations are pared away. Possible causes compete in unnervingly fine balance with each other.

Mitya's description works poetically: we understand his action not by analyzing his motive but rather through our willingness, along with his and Katerina Ivanovna's, to make symbolic associations. This is one of those passages in which we can see how much Freud learned or confirmed his own theories by reading Dostoevsky. At the moment of decision Mitya puts his forehead against the frozen pane ("the ice burned my forehead like fire"), then takes 5,000 rubles out of a book (he had received 6,000 rubles from his father as a final settlement), hands it to her, and makes her a deep bow. She gently returns him "a Russian bow, with her forehead to the floor," and runs away. He then draws his sword. "I drew it and nearly stabbed myself with it on the spot. . . . Can you understand that one might kill oneself with delight? But I didn't stab myself. I only kissed my sword and put it back in the scabbard—which there was no need to have told you, by the way" (*BK*, 103). It seems nearly an offense to art and to aesthetic pleasure to gloss such a passage, for it speaks so eloquently for itself. Suffice it to say, we have at last encountered those first two bows between Mitya and Katerina Ivanovna that hover behind and give significance to the multitude of bows that populate Part I. Now Mitya's desire to bow and to bow out to Katerina suggests a more resonant closure to their relationship than it had earlier.

Yet even as he confesses to Alyosha, Mitya falls prey to an even more insidious form of sensuality, the sensuality lurking in disclosure. "And I fancy that in telling you about my inner conflict I have laid it on rather thick to glorify myself" (*BK*, 103). Finally, although Mitya has settled upon one course of action—he cannot be insect, shopman, and man of honor all at once—because of the vividness and persuasiveness of his narration, all three still seem to exist simultaneously, particularly as they recede from the front of the reader's consciousness. He claims to have told "the whole truth just as it happened." That whole truth includes what did not happen as well as what did—that is, the potential as well as the actual. The border generated between the two is key: the specters of the insect and the shopman inform the action of the man of honor.

Mitya's genuine potential for taking any of these alternatives gives him the air of having taken all three. So he remains, perhaps even more so than before his confession, a character on the brink of calamity, a character who might behave abominably or honorably or, somehow, both. (This passage calls to mind *Crime and Punishment* [1865], in which Dostoevsky so exhaustively rehearsed all the possible motives for Raskolnikov's crime until they came to exist in a perfectly balanced competition with each other. In the course of writing that novel, Dostoevsky at first intended one particular motive to dominate, but as he himself increasingly could not decide which one should be uppermost, he threw up his hands and let the ultimate truth consist in that very multiplicity of motivation that he had initially hoped to move beyond.) Moreover, Mitya's actual course of action, honorable though it may have been, may be the most sensual of all.

By the end of this chapter readers have been put through their paces. The author has, in an unexpected way, shown his propensity for doubling. Rather than have one character "double" another—a standard technique for which Dostoevsky is exceedingly well known—he has employed a more subtle kind of doubling: the setting doubles a philosophical theme. The back alley dominates Mitya's confession geographically and morally; it is a feature of the narrator's description and of the character's worldview. Throughout the novel—and this is a feature of Dostoevsky's art in general—these unexpected doublings continue to arise and are the source, when we notice them, of pleasure—of the discovery of harmony amid seeming disarray, or as Mitya puts it, of "precious metal in the dirt."

Ever the self-conscious narrator, Mitya, as he begins the third part of his confession, shifts genres. "That half is a drama, and it was played out there. The second half is a tragedy, and it is being acted here" (*BK*, 104). Bakhtin has made axiomatic the notion that much of what is unique about Dostoevsky's fiction lies in his desire and ability to bring within the perimeters of the novel many kinds of discourse that are usually foreign to it (Bakhtin, 156–68, 203–4). Although Mitya does not really move beyond the expected discursive limits of a typical roman-tic hero, he does share his creator's taste for making (or at least claiming to make) rapid shifts in narrative stance. Chapters 3, 4, and 5 of Book III, taken together, demonstrate this shift. When we add Mitya's subse-quent actions to the stew, we find him intimately connected to yet another genre, the psychological thriller—a genre that Dostoevsky him-self, with *Crime and Punishment,* helped to create.

Where the "drama" section of Mitya's confession centers on the complexity of the mutual attraction and repulsion that he and Kate-rina Ivanovna feel for each other, the "tragedy" part focuses on money (particularly the 3,000 rubles that Katerina Ivanovna has just recently, in Skotoprigonevsk, entrusted to Mitya's care) and on the chaos that occurs when human relations become subject to the laws of the market-place. After Mitya had presented her with the 5,000 rubles, Katerina Ivanovna had become rich, with fairy-tale quickness, and declared her love for Mitya. In his reply to her, he puts in motion the tragedy. He falls from the lofty heights of a "man of honor": "One thing I shall be ashamed of forever. I referred to her being rich and having a dowry while I was only a stuck-up beggar! I mentioned money" (*BK*, 105).

Given the high, or low, romantic drama of Mitya's present situation—he would gladly be Grushenka's slave, "the porter at her gate," just as Katerina Ivanovna would be his—one would expect the tragedy to emerge from this volatile, overly charged situation. Yet Mitya sees his tragedy stemming instead from the violation he has committed upon his own honor. "Do you know, you innocent boy, that this is all delirium, senseless delirium, for there's a tragedy here. Let me tell you, Alexey, that I may be a low man, with low and degraded passions, but a thief and a pickpocket Dmitri Karamazov never can be. Well, then, let me tell you that I am a thief and a pickpocket" (*BK*, 107). He is more tormented by his squandering of Katerina Ivanovna's money than he is by his terrible treatment of her.

And it will be that 3,000 rubles that will reverberate so mightily throughout the story, that will lurk behind so many of Mitya's actions and behind their ramifications—from pulling the captain's beard to his subsequent frenzied visits around town. Although the traditional interpretations of Mitya tend to emphasize his unruliness and passion, it also becomes evident in this crucial chapter that Mitya's primary desire is to govern these impulses and to be a man of honor.

Finally, this last panel in the triptych of his confession reechoes and concretizes those motifs of the back alley that point both to his degradation and to his desire to escape it. Mitya becomes imbued with a sense that he is acting a part in a grand design. "The cycle of the ages is accomplished." And, "Destiny will be accomplished, and the best man will hold his ground while the undeserving one will vanish into his back alley forever—his filthy back alley, his beloved back alley. . . . It will be as I have said. I shall drown in the back alley, and she will marry Ivan." Yet even as he claims to use words "at random," Mitya modulates poetically from this persistent invocation of the back alley to the bow. "Say 'He bows to you.' . . . You must—you absolutely must—bow me out to her today" (*BK*, 106, 108).

The chapter closes with Mitya bringing to the surface yet another fundamental contradiction within himself: his fear that he will commit murder vies with his belief in miracles. Indeed, the force of the last page of this chapter is to create an atmosphere heavy with the expectation of a miracle. Yet again the minute parts of the novel replicate its whole, for the major thrust of Part I, from Alyosha's vantage point at least, is the expectation of a miracle upon Zosima's death.

The musical quality of Dostoevsky's prose, his tendency toward contrapuntal music, polyphony, and variations on themes, are nowhere more evident in his fiction than in *The Brothers Karamazov*. In the three chapters of Mitya's confession, with their interplay between the back alley and the bow, we can hear a single melody of Dostoevsky's "literary music." If this were an opera (it is at least, as we know, Mitya's "hymn of praise"), the back alley and the bow would be musical phrases characterizing Mitya.

IVAN

Dostoevsky used different strategies to introduce each brother into the novel. It is primarily the narrator-chronicler who relates anecdotes about Alyosha in preparation for our meeting with him, whereas Mitya tends to describe himself. For the first appearance of Ivan Fyodorovich, Dostoevsky used a different method entirely, one that he had used to powerful effect in *Crime and Punishment.* Our first real encounter with Ivan occurs through the explication of a text—an article he has recently written on the question of the ecclesiastical courts. Like most of the other ideas and motifs in this novel, Ivan's argument, as Father Iosif, the monastery's librarian, is quick to observe, "cuts both ways." (The literal translation from the Russian is "a stick with two ends.")

Even earlier, however, the narrator-chronicler had chosen to introduce Ivan to the reader through citing and briefly glossing his literary works. In fact, throughout much of the novel Ivan's biography quite simply is his bibliography: we learn about him through his fictional and nonfictional works. At the university Ivan had supported himself, in a manner reminiscent of the young Dostoevsky, through his efforts as a kind of feuilletonist, writing under the name "Eye Witness." His "interesting and piquant" paragraphs soon made him popular. Ivan then moved on to write "brilliant reviews," and at last, in his final year at the university, he gained a wider fame, even notoriety, through the publication of what the narrator-chronicler calls a "strange article," which both staunch members of the Church and atheists applauded, but which other "sagacious persons" considered to be a farce (*BK*, 11).

Thus Dostoevsky, through his narrator-chronicler, manages to give us simultaneously too much and too little information. Indeed, Ivan's article, in the absolute disagreement it provokes, sets him ahead of his time and renders him a thoroughly modern author whose texts inspire divergent deconstructions. Ivan tells Zosima that in his article he affirms that "the Church ought to include the whole State" rather than having a precise, well-defined position within it. The complicated, often abstruse conversation that follows shows the reader in no uncertain terms the difficulty of discerning what Ivan really thinks ("Ivan's a tomb," says Dmitri later), but it also gives Dostoevsky an opportunity to sound in yet another key a theme that has already been sounded in the novel in more comic form—especially through Fyodor's disquisition on the question of the hooks in hell—the question of crime and its punishment. Ivan, we are shortly to learn, is consumed with a hopeless, passionate desire for justice—for justice here on earth, and now.

The argument in his article possesses a seeming leniency: the

Church, were it to be all-powerful, would practice exclusion rather than execution. Yet Zosima is quick to realize that Ivan's argument in fact proposes an alternative of deadly severity. Ivan has quite simply deleted forgiveness and mercy from his scheme. Zosima agrees with him that earthly, temporal punishments seldom reform a criminal or deter a potential criminal, but he argues passionately against the excommunication of the criminal, however powerful and effective that punishment might be. "And what would become of the criminal, O Lord, if even the Christian society—that is, the Church—were to reject him even as the civil law rejects him and cuts him off?" (*BK*, 55)

Zosima here shows his theoretical hand as surely as Ivan has revealed his. Yet Zosima's words carry more than aphoristic weight, for even at this early juncture he has already offered forgiveness to a murderer, in the chapter "Peasant women who have faith." The Church's function, as Zosima sees it, is parental: it persists in "fatherly exhortation" of the criminal, and like a "tender, loving mother" offers comfort. Excommunication could provoke total despair and loss of faith (*BK*, 55–56).

Moreover, Father Paissy, "the silent and learned monk" (*BK*, 52), wonders if Ivan's article might in fact be a restatement and an affirmation of the third temptation of the devil, in which the Church is transformed into the State. Ivan seems to be arguing for the opposite, for the State's transformation into the Church, but the contours of his argument become hazy at this point. What is important, however, is that Dostoevsky has introduced into his novel the motif of the devil's three temptations to Jesus in the desert. This first sounding of the motif is emotionally uncharged; it will later become highly charged, deeply serious, and overladen with multiple layers of meaning.

In "Peasant women who have faith," Zosima had already demonstrated his commitment as an elder to fatherly exhortation and tender motherly love. This chapter sets up a dominant resonance for the whole novel (even as it stands in direct juxtaposition to another chapter in Part I, "The Controversy"). Before we have any real knowledge of the direction in which the plot for the Karamazov family might move, we encounter Zosima in his role as confessor to three peasant women. In a pattern typical of Dostoevsky's novels, this chapter seems at first to be a digression from the main story and a strategy to delay and prolong the mounting tension and the promise of scandalous action. It proves to be no digression but a prophetic first sounding and actual enactment of certain major themes.

Among a crowd of some twenty peasant women, Zosima speaks to five. During the course of this chapter, the narrator-chronicler assumes the guise of an eyewitness who allows himself to make a semi-autobiographical, semisociological digression. As the first peasant, "a possessed woman," is led up to Zosima, the narrator-chronicler remembers that, in his own childhood, he saw such women. He describes the evolution of his own understanding of this illness from an initial assumption that it was simulated to an acceptance of its terrible reality. His subsequent explanation of the power of the "holy sacrament" to momentarily dissolve this possession bears a strong resemblance to James's doctrine of the "will to believe." The woman's belief, "aroused by the expectation of the miracle of healing," actually causes a brief cure (*BK*, 39).

The narrator-chronicler's account of this faith healing has significant ramifications for the novel. Within this single paragraph we witness the narrator-chronicler's own changing outlook; we may be reminded of another possessed woman, Alyosha's mother; we watch Zosima bring about just such an episode of healing; finally, and most important, the narrator-chronicler directly sounds that dominant theme of the expectation of a miracle.

The second woman Zosima meets is "one from afar." This passage, as we have already seen, has a wrenching autobiographical significance. Into the language of this uneducated peasant woman Dostoevsky pours his own intimate, desperate grief for his dead child. The theme of the lost child is as important to Dostoevsky's entire literary canon as it is to that of Dickens. The outpouring of grief for a dead, injured, or suffering child constitutes the fundamental groundswell to this novel. Dostoevsky instilled in *The Brothers Karamazov* his own grief and love for his dead child, Alexey. He created a manly image of him in Alyosha; but in the characters of Ilyusha and his father—and here in the short vignette of the peasant woman and her dead three-year-old—he brought his own grief to life through fiction.

As Dostoevsky was beginning work on the novel, his Alyosha died. On the day of his son's death, Dostoevsky closed a letter to his brother Nikolai with the words, "Goodbye, Kolya, pity Lyosha. . . . I have never felt so sad."[9] Shortly thereafter, Anna Grigorievna sent her grieving husband, in the company of the philosopher Vladimir Solovyov, to the monastery of Optina Pustyn. The words of comfort uttered there to the bereaved, inconsolable Dostoevsky by the famous elder Father Amvrosy are echoed in Zosima's words to the peasant woman.

The real-life monk's words, spoken in private to Dostoevsky, are scattered like seeds in a fictional, created world where they take hardy root before reentering, by being read, the real world.

This passage also offers an excellent example of how Dostoevsky, by a quick shift in the texture of language and with a few deft strokes, can bring some readers to tears. If you found yourself ready to cry when you read this passage, it would perhaps be an interesting experiment to return to it and ask why. Does Dostoevsky manage to arouse our emotions without resorting to sentimentality? The bereft mother's language is full of repetitions, both of words and phrases—such as "my little boy"—and of ideas—"I can't forget him. He seems always standing before me. He never leaves me." She elaborates and enumerates while never for an instant wandering from her subject—her dead child. She encapsulates his preciousness through a litany of heart-wrenching synecdoches: "his little clothes, his little shirt, his little boots . . . all his little things." The repetitive, weaving, singsong, incantatory quality of her language brings us close to her grief. It brims with diminutives. When, in her great grief, she asks, not for her beloved child to return, but only to see him, from a distance, one more time, Dostoevsky indirectly conveys the infinitude of parental love.

> And if only I could look upon him one little time, if only I could peep at him one little time, without going up to him, without speaking, if I could be hidden in a corner and only see him one little minute, hear him playing in the yard, calling in his little voice, "Mummy, where are you?" If only I could hear him pattering with his little feet about the room just once, only once; for so often, so often I remember how he used to run to me and shout and laugh, if only I could hear his little feet I should know him! But he's gone, Father, he's gone, and I shall never hear him again. (*BK*, 41)

As she laments his death, she brings him poignantly to life for us. The image of this mother, whose entire being longs to hold her child again tight in an embrace and yet who asks only to see him from a distance pattering at play, strikes a keen nerve in the reader and conveys the essence of this novel.

Zosima first consoles her with conventional church wisdom. He tells her that her babe is rejoicing in the company of God and the angels. The woman is a believer; she has experienced no loss of faith, yet this answer offers her no comfort. Divine justice pales before the enormity of earthly injustice and loss. Thus, the peasant woman prefigures that complex rebellion against God's world that Ivan will shortly undergo.

Zosima quickly abandons standard church dogma and reaches into the biblical past and into the depths of his own heart to offer her counsel. "It is 'Rachel of old . . . weeping for her children and will not be comforted because they are not.' Such is the lot set on earth for you mothers. Be not comforted. Consolation is not what you need. Weep and be not consoled, but weep" (*BK*, 41–42). He urges her to remember, not to forget.

At this juncture another crucial prefiguring occurs, for Rachel's lost children remind us of those other lost and innocent ones smitten down by God—Job's children. Echoing the novel's epigraph, Zosima then assures her that her mother's grief will eventually modulate into quiet joy. We cannot accuse Dostoevsky of false piety here for the simple but irrefutable and irresistible fact that through her three-year-old Alexey he wrote of his own child. Thus in this short scene Dostoevsky has sounded, for the first time, the themes of the suffering and dying child whose death seems unjust and of the rebellion against God's world that can occur even without a loss of faith, as well as the themes evoked by the novel's epigraph. We have also seen how Dostoevsky can heat up his language and turn us into putty at a moment's notice.

Zosima's third encounter is with a peasant woman who has not heard from her son for a year. She is tempted to resort to superstition by offering up prayers for her son as though he were dead, in the hope that such a prayer would trouble his soul and cause him to write. Zosima chastises her, forgives her, and then predicts that her son will either write or return home very soon. "Your son is alive, I tell you" (*BK*, 43). Zosima's forecast proves to be correct, and some choose to regard it as a miracle of prediction. Thus this incident figures in the tension that operates throughout the novel between the dangerous assumption that a miracle will occur as predicted and the unexpected moments when it does in fact take place. Moreover, the incident as a whole calls to mind, as Terras has pointed out, the theme of the second temptation of Christ, for it is a rejection of magic and sorcery (Terras, *Karamazov Companion,* 148). All three of the devil's temptations will figure in Ivan's *Legend of the Grand Inquisitor.*

In his fourth encounter Zosima comforts a woman who confesses to him that she has murdered her husband. He assures her that God will forgive her and that she must think only of continual repentance. "If you are penitent, you love. And if you love, you are of God. All things are atoned for, all things are saved by love. If I, a sinner, even as you are, am tender with you and have pity on you, how much more will God" (*BK*, 44). Zosima, we will later learn, has already forgiven another murderer.

Finally Zosima meets a healthy peasant woman with her baby girl. She has come simply to see him, to bless him, and to ask him to give 60 kopecks to someone poorer than herself. We see Zosima receiving inspiration rather than giving it, although he then blesses the woman and her child. But this final encounter underscores the notion that Zosima himself is part of a chain of being in which we all nurture and are nurtured, love and are loved.

The entire chapter strongly recalls a similar pivotal chapter in *The Idiot* in which Myshkin tells Rogozhin of several faith-affirming encounters he has in two days with the Russian people. He too describes a murderer who maintains faith in God, and his last encounter is also with a mother who has a healthy baby in her arms. Both these peasant mothers operate almost as the concluding couplet of a sonnet: they send an illuminating shaft of meaning up through "the lines" that have preceded them. In this case, through the appearance of the mother who comes to Zosima simply to see him, Dostoevsky seems to be trying to show an actual moment of the "active love" that Zosima preaches.

Thus, this chapter that presents itself as a digression from the main action in fact prefigures and duplicates it. As such, it offers a compelling example of how Dostoevsky structured his work, how he balanced part and whole and wove a seamless web between them. For through his meetings with these five women, Zosima, in the space of a few short minutes, comes face to face with a possessed woman, with the grief felt at the death of a child, with superstition, with murder, and with the phenomenon of active love.

SMERDYAKOV

Like those of Fyodor Karamazov, Smerdyakov's theological questions absurdly and darkly parallel the dilemmas of the characters with whom we sympathize. Smerdyakov's beginnings are seemingly auspicious: he is the child of the *yurodivaya* "Stinking Lizaveta." At birth he was taken in as a foundling by Grigory and his wife Marfa after the loss of their own baby, so he becomes a kind of changling as well. "A child of God—an orphan is akin to all," Grigory had said, "and to us above others. Our little lost one has sent us this, who has come from the devil's son and a holy innocent. Nurse him and weep no more" (*BK*, 89).

But Grigory's tender emotions bear no fruit in Smerdyakov, and the reader will quickly come to despise this "little lost one." Although Grigory's words resonate powerfully with those of Zosima, their yield is a rotten one. Smerdyakov overflows with negative characteristics. From his name (connoting "stink") to his physical appearance, to his cynical—even sassy—theological disputations, he arouses nearly universal disgust.

Moreover, the night of his birth—which follows the day on which Grigory and Marfa had buried their baby—is filled with events that resurface with variations later in the novel. Like his probable half-brothers, Smerdyakov possesses several father figures, ranging from the devil to the faithful if intolerant Grigory—who had regarded his own six-fingered baby as a "dragon," "a confusion of nature" (*BK*, 85)—to the men who might be his biological father, Karp the convict, or Fyodor. Like Mitya, Smerdyakov evinces an affinity for the back alley; he is born in a bathhouse behind Fyodor's house, and he, not the poor dead child with six fingers, will prove to be the "confusion of nature."

After his baby's death, Grigory reads *The Lives of the Saints* and the Book of Job. Then, just as will occur shortly in Part II, Marfa hears sounds that awaken her. She awakens Grigory, who runs to the garden, as he will again in Part II. The garden gate is locked. Grigory's first nighttime foray into the garden occurs at Smerdyakov's birth; his next foray will mark an even more momentous event, also one occasioned by Smerdyakov. Smerdyakov will come to have a dual role in the novel. Both figuratively and literally he will be both lackey and tempter, or devil. Like Fyodor, he makes an ominous yet comic attempt to pit reason against the divine justice of God's world.

It is interesting to note that the narrator-chronicler likens Smerdyakov to the peasant in the painting *Contemplation* by the Russian artist Kramskoy. This peculiar passage at the end of the chapter "Smerdyakov" resonates negatively with the novel's epigraph. Later in the novel Zosima warns that evil seeds can take root as well as good ones: a passing spiteful remark to a child can lodge in the child's heart with disastrous results. (Perhaps Grigory's angry words to Smerdyakov are a case in point: " 'Are you a human being,' he said, addressing the boy directly. 'You're not a human being. You grew from the mildew in the bathhouse' " [BK, 112].) The narrator-chronicler reads the face of Kramskoy's peasant as that of someone who is hoarding unconscious impressions. That peasant could go off on a pilgrimage to Jerusalem, or set fire to his village, or do both. Dostoevsky thus loaded Smerdyakov with a dramatic potential as heightened as that with which he endowed his brothers.

At the age of 12 Smerdyakov, during a lesson in the Scripture, suddenly grinned, then asked, "God created light on the first day, and the sun, moon and stars on the fourth day. Where did the light come from on the first day?" (BK, 112). Moreover, as a child he had dressed up as a priest and "with great ceremony" buried cats that he had himself previously hung. Smerdyakov's childhood activities and questions resemble nothing so much as Ivan's own questions, though in parodic and belittled form. Smerdyakov's pomp and ceremony over the bodies of his own victims likewise prefigures the activity of Ivan's Grand Inquisitor. Ivan and his Grand Inquisitor will soon move us with their discourse; when they do, we must look back to the angry antics of the young Smerdyakov and consider the affinities between the two lofty figures and the disgusting youngster. Add to this mix the fact that it is Smerdyakov whom Dostoevsky chose to endow with epilepsy. As Gary Saul Morson has pointed out, Smerdyakov's passion for evil is motiveless. It thus links him with Shakespeare's Iago.[10] Dostoevsky knew his Shakespeare well and in a different context would later mention *Othello* (BK, 358).

In the chapter "The Controversy" Smerdyakov indulges in cynical observations about a soldier who, as reported in a recent newspaper article, had refused to renounce Christianity and embrace Islam while under torture and had subsequently been flayed alive.[11] Smerdyakov's opinions recapitulate in comic yet profoundly negative terms much that has gone before. He suggests that the soldier should have "in that emergency" renounced his faith and then later expiated his sin by good works (BK, 116). This proposition, at first glance, does not seem so different from Zosima's assurances to the woman who has murdered her husband that she can expiate her sin through love and forgiveness. Yet one proposition is a demonic temptation to evil and the other a description of how to enact a genuine repentance. Dostoevsky is asking us to begin making these spiritual distinctions before the main action of the novel has even begun.

Smerdyakov, likewise, is the first to raise the philosophical question that each of the brothers must eventually face: Where is the ethical boundary between thought and deed? At what point does thought become deed? He speculates that were he the soldier in question he would have done well to curse God before his Islamic torturers, for at "that very instant, not only when I say it aloud, but when I think of saying it, before a quarter of a second has passed, I am cut off." And then, he reasons, if by having this thought he ceased to be a Christian, he would no longer be lying to his enemies in claiming his renunciation. And if he would no longer be a Christian, "with what sort of justice can I then be held responsible?" (*BK,* 116, 117).

Dostoevsky scathingly indicts, through Smerdyakov, the kind of reasoning applied to theological issues that he believed to be typical of the Jesuits, whom he despised. Fyodor chastises Smerdyakov, "Ah, you casuist. He must have been with the Jesuits somewhere, Ivan. Oh, you stinking Jesuit, who taught you?" (*BK,* 118). (The irony, of course, is that Smerdyakov has been "with" Ivan; Ivan has taught him.) Moreover, Smerdyakov, like Fyodor, uses reason and his own sense of earthly justice to counter the tenets of Christian faith, not from the perspective of an atheist but as a believer. When Fyodor paraphrases the Bible and claims, like the devil, to be "the father of lies," he is, literally, the father of the lying and demonic—though pettily so—Smerdyakov.

Finally, in his antiparable (Matt. 17:20 and 21:21), Smerdyakov ferociously takes on the interlaced questions of faith, miracles, and the expectation of miracles. His words stand in counterpoint to those of Zosima in the "Peasant women" chapter and are the third reference in the novel to the devil's temptations of Jesus. Thus his commentary is yet another heralding of Ivan's upcoming poem of the Grand Inquisitor. Smerdyakov taunts the faithful servant Grigory: "It is said in the Sacraments that if you have faith, even as a mustard seed, and bid a mountain move into the sea, it will move without the least delay at your bidding." (Here is another variation on the epigraph—a dissonant one.) "Well . . . you try yourself telling this mountain not to move into the sea, for that's a long way off sir, but even to our stinking little river which runs at the bottom of the garden. You'll see for yourself, sir, that it won't budge, but will remain just where it is, however much you shout at it" (*BK,* 118).

As an afterthought Smerdyakov speculates that there are probably one or two people "somewhere in the Egyptian desert" who could make the mountain move. But would God really curse all the rest? This curious conclusion is part of the strange chain of associations that links Smerdyakov, Zosima, the Grand Inquisitor, and, much later, Ivan's devil: Zosima had earlier referred to Acts 6:3, "the seven righteous men" on whom Christian society rests. (Note, too, that on the very same page, Father Paissy had referred to the devil's third temptation [*BK*, 57].) The Grand Inquisitor, a Jesuit, later alludes to the same notion of the seven righteous men and speaks of the eating of "roots in the desert" (*BK*, 242); the devil puts forth his three temptations to Jesus in the desert; and Ivan's hallucinatory devil, toward the end of the novel, reveals his own special arithmetic, which places the highest value on those righteous hermits dining on locusts in the desert and praying for the souls of mankind.

In typical fashion, Fyodor shrewdly and with relish goes to the heart of the matter: "So you do suppose there are two who can move mountains? Ivan, make a note of it, write it down. There you have the Russian soul all over" (*BK*, 119). Thus, both the narrator-chronicler, through his observations about Kramskoy's painting, and Fyodor have alerted us that the darkness, obscurity, and rebellion emanating from Smerdyakov are somehow quintessentially Russian. Moreover, Ivan does indeed, at least unconsciously, make note of Smerdyakov's words, as we shall see later when his devil, speaking about just such matters, explains the principles of his demonic arithmetic.

This scene climaxes in Mitya's first blow to Grigory and his physical attack on his father. These events function as a rehearsal of the events of the next evening. "If I haven't killed him, I'll come again and kill him," Mitya shouts. Alyosha at last leaves his father's house to return to the monastery. As he crosses the yard he sees Ivan "sitting on the bench at the gateway. He was sitting writing something in pencil in his notebook" (*BK*, 130). Although it is customary and accurate to regard Ivan as Smerdyakov's teacher and Smerdyakov as Ivan's lackey, Smerdyakov is also, in his role as tempter and devil, Ivan's teacher. Later ("tomorrow," in the novel), in Ivan's poem, we do see, though in far more elevated form, a reworking of precisely the elements in Smerdyakov's parable about the soldier and faith. As Terras has pointed out, Dostoevsky may also be alluding, as he so often did in his literary and journalistic polemics, to the Russian radical Nikolai Chernyshevsky and his novel *What Is to Be Done?* (1863), in which seven "reliable followers" are claimed for the socialist movement (Terras, *Karamazov Companion*, 153). As with the other dominant symbols and ideas in this novel, the notion of the righteous few cuts both ways.

The disputations of Fyodor Pavlovich and Smerdyakov are, with their deliberate and unconscious humor, associated with the devil. "Who is laughing at mankind, Ivan?" asks Fyodor. "It must be the devil," he replies, although Ivan quickly goes on to assert, unconvincingly, his lack of faith in both God and the devil (*BK*, 122).

Alyosha's day is not yet over. During his visit wtih Katerina Ivanovna the extraordinary scene between her and Grushenka takes place, and he meets Mitya yet again at the crossroads. He returns to the monastery and at last opens the note from Lise Khokhlakova, which contains a declaration of love. Part I concludes with Alyosha's prayers and his "peaceful sleep." Along the way, the reader has already undergone an intense, though often humorous, spiritual excursion. The narrator-chronicler has given important clues to the suspense thriller that is taking shape. Most important, the novel has begun to ask its difficult questions about the nature of confession, the meaning of faith, the function of miracle, the right of people to judge and forgive each other, the place of reason in explaining the mysteries of the human heart, and the obligations of parents and children to each other. All of these questions, moreover, have already begun to intersect and collide with each other.

From this point on, as we move through the novel, I shall stop only at those points where the tangle becomes most intense. By the end of this first day in the narrator's chronicle the reader has entered deeply into the world of Skotoprigonevsk. It is a world that is confined yet full of ramifications that spread beyond its borders. The reader has begun the arduous, deeply associative task of moving through a dense, yet fluid medium in which "all things are connected."

5

The Deep Heart's Core
PART II: BOOKS IV, V, AND VI

Part II extends through the second day of the action of the novel. By now, as with any successful work of art, the reader has entered a structural domain in which the relationship between signifier and signified is different from what is in the real world: such details as bad odors, bad breath, kisses, stones, and bitten fingers become resonant semantic tags for the metaphysical and ethical paradoxes Dostoevsky explores.

BOOK IV

The theme of laceration (*nadryv*) hovers over Book IV and provides a thread of continuity among characters who are otherwise diverse: the hermit monk Father Ferapont, Katerina Ivanovna, Lise Khokhlakova, Captain Snegiryov, and Ivan. The action of Book IV, like that of Books II and III, is organized around the movements of Alyosha, who continues—a literal ficelle—to tie the action together.

Yet Alyosha's visits now encompass a wider sphere: the world of Captain Snegiryov, his son Ilyusha, the schoolboy Kolya Krasotkin, and the other schoolboys expands the novel's field of action and serves to underline Zosima's religious pronouncement that everything is connected to everything else in the great ocean of being. Moreover, Dostoevsky was carrying out a primary intention of his own. Before he started work on the novel, he had written, in March 1878, "I have been planning and will soon start writing a long novel in which, among other things, a considerable part will be played by children, and specifically young children from the ages of about 7 to 15" (*Letters,* 448).

Old Karamazov had used Snegiryov as an agent to reclaim Mitya's IOUs. In anger, Mitya had rushed to the tavern and pulled the captain's beard. Through this incident the reader enters upon a situation so compelling that it could easily assume center stage, with the Karamazov family problems serving as a mere backdrop. Here we see Dostoevsky's penchant for creating doubles—second-tier characters representing aspects or potentials of the main character. Yet these second-tier characters quickly assume a full-fledged independence of their own. This will be especially true of Kolya Krasotkin, although this dual novelistic function as both modifier and subject applies to the captain and his son Ilyusha as well.

Belknap offers the most complete and concise discussion of the *nadryv* as it operates in *The Brothers Karamazov.* He links it to buffoonery—already associated with Fyodor Karamazov and the ridiculous hanger-on Maximov—another theme with which it overlaps. To *nadryv,* Belknap observes, belongs the tragic sense of the absurd. "Just as buffoonery was a twisted response to poverty and blows received, so the *nadryv* is a twisted response to wealth and benefits received, or at least offered. . . . In this sense the *nadryv* is the exact opposite of buffoonery—involving pride, riches, dignity, and a pressing fear of being base while the buffoon embodies humiliation, poverty, shame, and pursuit of baseness" (Belknap, 46).

Yet he also points out that, despite their oppositions, the *nadryv* and buffoonery are two extremes along the same axis. This axis embodies "perversity, willfulness, self-consciousness, self-dramatization, and absurdity" (Belknap, 46). Thus a chain begins to emerge with such otherwise widely diverging characters as the captain, Fyodor, Mitya, Lise, Father Ferapont, Katerina Ivanovna, and Ivan serving as links. The perversity or willfulness of one of these characters can generate a similar set of responses in another. It is not for nothing that Alyosha, toward daybreak on the previous night, had half woken up calling out "Laceration, laceration" (*BK,* 170). A laceration, as we see throughout Book IV, is a wound inflicted upon oneself out of a twisted pride that may also thus seek, indirectly, to hurt others.

Another axis slices through Book IV, a spiritual axis expressed in a poetic cluster revolving around bread and stones. Its poles involve pride and pain on one end and love and spiritual nourishment on the other. The opening chapter of Book IV, "Father Ferapont," displays both these axes and contains ominous foreshadowings of upcoming events. First, from a letter to Alyosha borne by Rakitin from Lise's mother, Madame Khokhlakova (two unbelievers), we learn of Zosima's "miracle of prediction" of the day before, a miracle that feeds the general expectation that something even greater will happen upon the occasion of Zosima's imminent death.

Contrasted to Zosima is Father Ferapont—the ascetic, mad monk who dislikes Zosima and is given to fasting and visions of devils. The visiting monk from Obdorsk voices his admiration for Ferapont: "All the year round, even at Easter, you take nothing but bread and water, and what we should eat in two days lasts you a full seven. It's truly marvelous—your great abstinence" (*BK*, 153). Ferapont, by his minimal intake of earthly bread, hopes, in his pride, to mimic Christ and to recall the moment when the devil tried to tempt Jesus to turn the stones into bread. Jesus had replied that man lives not by bread alone—that spiritual bread was more valuable to Him than earthly bread and that men's faith could not be bought by such measures. However much Dostoevsky revered this biblical moment, he is quick to parody and undercut Ferapont's trite imitation of it. Through Ferapont, Dostoevsky ridicules the assumption that simple abstinence from earthly bread is itself an indication of an abundance of spiritual bread.

" 'And mushrooms?' asked Father Ferapont suddenly. 'Mushrooms?' repeated the surprised monk. 'Yes. I can give up their bread, not needing it at all, and go away into the forest and live there on the mushrooms or the berries, but they can't give up their bread here, wherefore they are in bondage to the devil' " (*BK*, 153). Ferapont's unexpected emphasis on mushrooms, which he cannot give up, as opposed to bread, which he can, suggests that he has simply replaced one earthly appetite with another—one that, moreover, carries with it the connotation of hallucination. Indeed, Ferapont's subsequent descriptions of his demonic visions resemble nothing so much as Ivan's hallucinatory vision of his devil. Thus, the giving up of earthly bread can be as much associated with the temptations of the devil as wanting it can be. Again we see how Dostoevsky makes his themes cut both ways.

Ferapont says that he quickly slammed the door and pinched the tip of the devil's tail in it. "He squealed and started to struggle, and I made the sign of the cross over him three times. And he died on the spot like a crushed spider. He must have rotted there in the corner and be stinking" (*BK,* 154). Ferapont's lacerating words will find numerous echoes in the events to come: Lise slams her own finger in the door; the Karamazov sensuality is spiderlike; Zosima's dead body stinks mightily. Although Ferapont imagines that he communicates with the Holy Ghost, the reader realizes that he is more likely communicating with the devil.

Counterposed to these dark forebodings is Zosima's assurance to Alyosha that he shall not die without making certain that Alyosha hears his "last word. To you I will say that word, my son, it will be my last gift to you" (*BK,* 155). The demonic Ferapont is silent for days at a time; the holy Zosima's words flow freely. They are "gifts," or, as the novel's epigraph suggests, seeds. Yet in Ivan's poem the Grand Inquisitor has many words to utter, while Jesus remains silent. As always in Dostoevsky's metaphysical schema, boundaries shift, polarities crumble, and each powerful motif—in this case, words versus silence—can cut both ways. Likewise, in the next chapter Fyodor's last words (forever) to Alyosha are about the fish soup he plans to serve up to his youngest son the next day. This continues the play between physical nourishment—fish soup—and spiritual nourishment—Zosima's promised "last word."

As we saw earlier, the third chapter of Book I—"Peasant women who have faith"—constituted a seeming digression or delay in the main action but proved, in fact, to be central to the structure of the plot. Now the third chapter of Book IV, "A Meeting with the schoolboys," functions identically: it too seems to be a digression. Alyosha has left his father's house and is rushing to Madame Khokhlakova's, hoping to find Dmitri as well. Instead, "an incident" occurs that delays him: he witnesses the stone throwing between Ilyusha and the other schoolboys.

Alyosha stops to talk to the group of boys by the bridge, all of whom have stones in their hands, and sees another boy standing some 30 paces away. Alyosha, who had just unknowingly kissed his father on the shoulder for the last time, is suddenly struck on his shoulder by a stone. As he tries to defend his assailant, who turns out to be Ilyusha, he is hit several more times. Finally Ilyusha bites Alyosha's finger to the bone. Alyosha binds his finger and says, "Though I don't know you . . . yet I must have done something to you. . . . How have I wronged you, tell me?" (*BK,* 164). Ilyusha breaks into tears and runs off; Alyosha continues on his way.

Moreover, the next chapter follows a pattern similar to chapter 4 of Book I; each focuses on Madame Khokhlakova and her daughter and seems to be central to the main action but is in fact peripheral. Alyosha leaves her house with 200 rubles for Snegiryov from Katerina Ivanovna. He realizes that the child who bit him must be the captain's son. As he walks along he pulls out a roll and eats it. This bread makes him "feel stronger" (*BK,* 179). When Alyosha visits the Snegiryov family he repeatedly assures them that Dmitri will beg forgiveness publicly for his insult. "He will bow down at your feet in the middle of the marketplace" (*BK,* 187). Readers of *Crime and Punishment* know that in Dostoevsky's view such an act is a mighty gesture of contrition.

By this point, Ilyusha's sufferings seem unbearably unfair. Desperate with fear, he has publicly begged Dmitri, the tormentor, to forgive his father, the victim. Since then he has borne the insults and injuries of the boys whose affection is so precious to him. He has begged his father, to no avail, to avenge himself. He has had to learn that the romantic, honorable solution of a duel offers no solution at all to the impoverished head of an ailing family. These psychic lacerations make the physical injury—from being struck above the heart by a stone—seem minor.

Suddenly the language of the novel makes the same leap into sublime and piercing emotion that we heard in the words of the peasant mother whose baby had died. Now a poor father's words of anguish over the unjust sufferings of his child lacerate our hearts:

> An ordinary boy, a weak son, would have submitted, have felt ashamed of his father, sir, but he stood up for his father against them all. For his father and for truth and justice, sir. For what he suffered when he kissed your brother's hand and cried to him "forgive daddy, forgive daddy"—that only God knows—and I, sir, his father. . . . But at that moment in the square, when he kissed his hand, at that moment my Ilyushka had grasped all that justice means, sir. That truth entered into him and crushed him forever, sir. (*BK,* 188)

The truth's power to crush and injure is greater than that of any stone. We are shortly, in Book V, to encounter another innocent child who pleads hopelessly for forgiveness. But the truth's power to nourish is also greater than that of any bread. Once again, the dominant images cut both ways.

Moreover, the language of this passage resembles that of the peasant woman. Both she and Snegiryov describe a scene so vividly that it comes completely to life; both use many diminutives and much repetition. Snegiryov's use of the word *sir* embodies the anguish and ambivalence of his own laceration. He calls Alyosha "sir" out of both respect and contempt. In each use of the word one emotion may outweigh the other; but both are present, and together they constitute his laceration: the word lacerates both ways.

The power of truth and stones to injure is counterbalanced in this scene by their power to heal as well. As Snegiryov recites the agonizing truth to Alyosha, they are approaching "that great stone" (*BK*, 189) to which the captain and Ilyusha are in the habit of going in the evening. It is a place where they can speak the truth to each other. As Snegiryov and Alyosha reach the comforting (spiritually nourishing) stone, Snegiryov's anguish and the power of his words reach their apex. He describes how the night before he and Ilyusha had "reached the stone where we are now." They had watched some kites flying, and the captain had offered to mend theirs.

> My boy made no answer. . . . He suddenly fell on me, threw both his little arms around my neck and held me tight. You know, when children are silent and proud, and try to keep back their tears when they are in great trouble and suddenly break down, their tears fall in streams, sir. With those warm streams of tears, sir, he suddenly wetted my face. . . . "daddy," he kept crying, "daddy, darling daddy, how he insulted you! Daddy," he said, "daddy." "Ilyusha," I said to him, "Ilyusha darling." No one saw us then, sir. God alone saw us. I hope he will enter it on my service record, sir. (*BK*, 190)

Even as Snegiryov's lacerating, confessional lament disintegrates into buffoonery, as it must, we remain confronted with a scene of incredible intimacy and pain; Ilyusha's tears simultaneously nourish and wound us—not unlike the stones that have so dominated Book IV ("Lacerations"). With a digression from the main action like this one, who needs a main plot?

BOOK V

The next section of *The Brothers Karamazov*, Book V ("Pro and Contra"), presented Dostoevsky with special conflicts between his tasks as an artist and as a believing Christian, for it is here that Ivan, through his magnificent poem in prose, *The Legend of the Grand Inquisitor,* puts forth the terms of his rebellion against God and His ordering of the world. It is this section of the novel that has most consistently gripped Dostoevsky's readers and that Dostoevsky himself knew was the heart of the matter. On 10 May 1879 he wrote from Staraya Russa to his editor, N. A. Lyubimov:

> This fifth book is in my view the culminating point of the novel and must be finished with particular care. Its meaning, as you will see from the text I sent, is the depiction of extreme blasphemy and the kernel of the idea of destruction of our time, in Russia. . . . My hero chooses a theme I consider irrefutable: the absurdity of all historical reality. I don't know whether I executed it well but I know the figure of my hero is a real one to the utmost degree. . . . Everything my hero says in the text I sent you is based on reality. All the anecdotes about children took place, existed, were published in the press. . . . I invented nothing. . . . My hero's blasphemy will be triumphantly refuted in the next (June) issue, on which I am now working with fear, trembling, and veneration. (*BK,* 758)

The paradoxes embedded in his letter virtually leap off the page: he considers the argument upon which Ivan bases his rebellion to be irrefutable, yet he sets out to refute it. It is usual, when reading *The Brothers Karamazov,* to discover the indirect means Dostoevsky brings to bear in this monumental task of refuting Ivan's arguments, both in the words of Zosima's last exhortations and in the rapidly ensuing events of the novel. Yet a close reading of Book V suggests yet another way Dostoevsky deviously refutes Ivan's argument: he uses the words and emotions of Ivan himself. By the end of *The Brothers Karamazov* the reader may decide that Ivan has undergone or is at least in the midst of a genuine spiritual conversion.[1] For we can argue that it is Ivan himself who offers up the most compelling counterpoint to his own objections. The dialogic nature of this novel expresses itself powerfully through the competing and conflicting ideas and actions of its characters, but even more compelling are the dialogisms and polyphonies that exist within single characters, and within single thoughts. The words of Xenos Clark, an obscure American philosopher, so aptly quoted by William James, spring to mind—"The truth is that we travel on a journey that was accomplished before we set out."[2]

Numerous real-life sources exist for Ivan, from the Russian philosopher Vladimir Solovyov to the great Russian radical Vissarion Belinsky. But Dostoevsky's hero, like all the Karamazovs, without exception, is also profoundly autobiographical; perhaps those seeds of Ivan's regeneration, evident in him even at the very moment of his most dramatic renunciation, emanate from the part of him most intimately related to Dostoevsky but transformed by his art. After all, more than 25 years earlier Dostoevsky had written hauntingly to Madame N. D. Fonvizina, the wife of the Decembrist Mikhail Fonvizin, of his own spiritual condition:

> And not because you are religious, but because I myself have experienced it and felt it, I shall tell you that at such a time one thirsts for faith as "the withered grass" thirsts for water, and one actually finds it, because in misfortune the truth shines through. I can tell you about myself that I am a child of this century, a child of doubt and disbelief, I have always been and shall ever be (that I know), until they close the lid of my coffin. What terrible torment this thirst to believe has cost me and is still costing me, and the stronger it becomes in my soul, the stronger are the arguments against it. And, despite all this, God sends me moments of great tranquillity, moments during which I love and am loved by others; and it was during such a moment that I found within myself a symbol of faith in which all is clear and sacred for me. This symbol is very simple, and here is what it is: to believe that there is nothing more beautiful, more profound, more sympathetic, more reasonable, more courageous, and more perfect than Christ; and there not only isn't, but I tell myself with a jealous love, there cannot be. More than that—if someone succeeded in proving to me that Christ was outside the truth, and if, *indeed*, the truth was outside Christ, I would sooner remain with Christ than with the truth. (*Letters*, 68)

"Pro and Contra" is indisputably Ivan's book, yet if we look closely, it is Alyosha who, for most of it, is depressed and embarking upon the spiritual crisis that will reach its decisive moment in his own book, Book VII, "Alyosha." He laments to Lise that his brothers are destroying themselves and others with them. "It's 'the primitive force of the Karamazovs,' as Father Paissy said the other day. . . . Does the spirit of God move above that force? Even that I don't know. I only know that I, too, am a Karamazov. . . . And perhaps I don't even believe in God" (*BK*, 202).

We tend to view Alyosha's spiritual crisis as emanating either from the eloquence and persuasiveness of Ivan's upcoming description of the unjustified sufferings of children (his "Rebellion") or from the despairing bitterness and grief Alyosha experiences when Zosima's dead body begins to stink. Yet Alyosha's crisis, these words show us, had already begun before the events that we often attribute it to even occur. Moreover, Alyosha continues in the role that has already been his throughout the novel: he travels the streets and alleys on various missions; he continues, in vain, to hunt for Mitya; he eventually finds Ivan instead.

By three o'clock on the second day of the narrative the sense "that a great inevitable catastrophe was about to happen" has begun to weigh Alyosha down. The narrator-chronicler tells us that Alyosha is "very depressed—depressed by suspense and uncertainty" (*BK*, 205). Thus this sense of impending catastrophe counterbalances the equally powerful expectation of an upcoming miracle. Indeed, a catastrophe possesses, in certain respects, the characteristics of a miracle—in negative form. Each is cataclysmic; each changes one's sense of what precedes and succeeds it.

Alyosha happens upon Smerdyakov, who, as he had already done in Book III, prefigures in grotesque form the ideas that will shortly sound with complete seriousness. He functions here as a true lackey, possessing a "lackey's tenor and lackey's song" (*BK*, 205); by the end of Book V he stands ready at the gate for Ivan, both as his physical lackey and as the lackey of Ivan's soul. Alyosha overhears Smerdyakov, who has just been singing a rhymed song, tell the silly former maidservant Marya Kondratyevna, "Poetry is rubbish. . . . Consider yourself, who ever talks in rhyme?" (*BK*, 208). This remark coarsely foreshadows Ivan shyly, even touchingly calling his poem in prose "a ridiculous thing" (*BK*, 227).

Moreover, moments before Ivan begins his narrative he voices his rebellion to Alyosha with the conclusion (later picked up by the French existentialists), "And so I hasten to give back my entrance ticket" (*BK*, 226). Yet this powerful moment has also been parodied and distorted already by Smerdyakov: "I would have sanctioned their killing me before I was born that I might not have come into the world at all, ma'am" (*BK*, 206). Ivan calls the ideas of Europe "a most precious graveyard" (*BK*, 212); Smerdyakov thinks, "it would have been a good thing if they [the French led by Napoleon] had conquered us" (*BK*, 206). Ivan acknowledges that Russians frequently evince a "peculiar" satisfaction in the inflicting of pain (*BK*, 221); Smerdyakov concludes, "I hate all Russia" (*BK*, 206). Smerdyakov responds to Alyosha's questions about Dmitri's whereabouts with a quiet and unnerving paraphrase of Gen. 4:9 ("And the Lord said unto Cain, where is Abel thy brother? And he said, I know not: Am I my brother's keeper?"): "How am I to know. . . . It's not as if I were his keeper" (*BK*, 208). Smerdyakov here loudly sounds the theme of the repudiation of responsibility that Ivan will reecho three times during the course of Book V.

Each of Ivan's ideas bristles with complexity and ambivalence; Smerdyakov's are simple, flat, concrete. Ivan laughs at Alyosha and tells him, "It's wonderful how you can turn words, as Polonius says in *Hamlet*. . . . You turn my words against me. Well, I am glad" (*BK*, 220). Alyosha does indeed "turn Ivan's words" and in doing so uncovers the seed of grace lurking at their heart. But Smerdyakov, another "turner of words," functions in precisely the opposite way—truly turning Ivan's words against him, literalizing and enacting their evil kernel. In each case the word itself, like a seed, is an agent both for evil and for good.

From the moment Alyosha joins Ivan at his table in the Metropolis Tavern their conversation takes on an aura of heady biblical and metaphysical import, tempered by everyday reality. Their talk about food (fish soup, cherry jam)—"You don't live by tea alone, I suppose" (*BK*, 210)—prefaces Ivan's upcoming tale of the Grand Inquisitor and reflects Alyosha's own Karamazov thirst for life: "I am hungry" (*BK*, 210).

Moreover, Alyosha paraphrases, even plagiarizes—as he has done before and will do again shortly—the ideas of others: he tells Ivan that he is a riddle, thereby echoing Mitya's pronouncements about both the human condition in general ("God sets us nothing but riddles") and Ivan in particular ("Ivan is a tomb") (*BK*, 97, 99). Though Mitya is absent, both Ivan and Alyosha had hoped to find him, and his shadow hovers over the ensuing chapter. Moreover, Ivan's upcoming confession to Alyosha even shares certain features with Dmitri's tripartite confession to Alyosha in Book III.

Ivan initiates his rebellion, which will shortly erupt into a devastating litany of the sufferings of children, with a passionate acknowledgment of his youthful "greenness" and his "perhaps unseemly thirst for life" (*BK*, 211). Mitya had also told Alyosha that within the very depths of his degradation he could not resist singing a "hymn of praise"; he too had felt that joy "without which the world cannot stand" (*BK*, 96). Each brother realizes that this Karamazovian thirst for life is not completely base. Ivan, echoing the words of one of Dostoevsky's famous dreamers, the speaker of "The Dream of a Ridiculous Man" (1877), explains that this thirst for life is not base because it is what creates the desire to live when logic might suggest otherwise. "Though I may not believe in the order of the universe, yet I love the sticky little leaves as they open in spring" (*BK*, 211).

In fact, Ivan and Alyosha virtually paraphrase Dostoevsky's "ridiculous man" in their conversation. Their words are emblematic of a belief cherished by Dostoevsky, a belief that he sought in each of his novels to portray, however indirectly. " 'I am awfully glad that you have such a longing for life,' cried Alyosha. 'I think everyone should love life above everything in the world.' 'Love life more than the meaning of it?' 'Certainly, love it, regardless of logic, as you say, it must be regardless of logic, and it's only then one will understand the meaning of it' " (*BK*, 212). Like Dmitri, Ivan totters on the brink between salvation and disaster.

All three brothers share an acute sense of this impending metaphysical crisis. Curiously, both Dmitri and Ivan assure Alyosha, who is simultaneously seeking to reassure each of them, that all is not lost. Mitya says, "Alyosha, I believe in miracles" (*BK*, 110), and Ivan exclaims, "You are trying to save me, but perhaps I am not lost" (*BK*, 212). Nevertheless, each brother feels the insectlike Karamazov presence within himself, the dark side of that thirst for life. "I am a bug," asserts Mitya; "I am a bug," asserts Ivan (*BK*, 102, 224).

Ivan's subsequent compelling denunciation of the order of God's world cries out to be read in tandem with his instinctive love for life, for the sticky leaves, for his own greenness. Ironically, it is Dmitri who, more or less rationally, describes that battlefield in the heart of man. It is Ivan who wanders lost upon it. Another of Dostoevsky's stories, "A Gentle Creature" (1876), closes with a cry of pain that rings with the same emotional density as Ivan's outpouring, " 'Is there a living man on the plain?' cries the Russian legendary hero. I, too, echo the same cry, but no one answers."[3]

Mitya, echoing Dostoevsky's own beliefs about *pochvennichestvo*, exclaims, "But the difficulty is how am I to cling forever to Mother Earth. I don't kiss her; I don't cleave her bosom. . . . I am in tears" (*BK*, 96). Like Mitya, Ivan imagines that he, upon visiting that "precious graveyard" of Europe, would likewise cling to the earth. "I know I shall fall on the ground and kiss those stones and weep over them" (*BK*, 212). Neither act occurs; both are passionately desired.

When Alyosha meets Dmitri, the latter has been drinking. Likewise Ivan, by the time Alyosha joins him in the tavern, has finished dinner and is drinking tea. The narrator-chronicler describes the usual tavern bustle, which includes the sound of bottles being opened, but we do not know if Ivan has been drinking, too. Nevertheless, each brother confesses to Alyosha in an atmosphere charged by the presence of alcohol; each brother talks about coincidence (*BK*, 93, 211); each declares his love for Alyosha (*BK*, 93, 249); each realizes that, despite the spiritual nourishment offered by that love, he stands at a boundary, the crossing of which will alter life forever (*BK*, 143, 258–59).

Only after Ivan's affirmation of his belief in God, his declaration of his love for life, and his vital admission that he might in fact not "be lost" does his rebellion come. How, then, are we to understand it? Is his rebellion made more forceful, poignant, and meaningful by the powerful statements of affirmation preceding it, or is it undercut by them? Dmitri had envisioned mankind as a riddle; Alyosha thinks of Ivan as a riddle; and we, the readers, come face to face with both a general and a specific riddle as we try to understand these chapters.

Early on in the novel Fyodor had mused about the likelihood of the existence of hooks on the ceiling of hell. Now at last we come up against an instance of reason being counterposed against God's world that has nothing of the comic or parodic about it. Ivan speaks of those philosophers "who dare to dream that two parallel lines, which according to Euclid can never meet on earth, may meet somewhere in infinity" (*BK*, 216). He then proceeds to set up a metaphysical equation to illustrate the upcoming terms of his rebellion:

$$\frac{\text{non-Euclidean geometry}}{\text{Euclidean geometry}} = \frac{\text{God's justice}}{\text{earthly justice}}$$

Terras points out that this equation "works against Ivan because there *is* such a thing as non-Euclidean geometry" (Terras, *Karamazov Companion*, 129). But it is crucial that we acknowledge that Ivan himself is the one who suggests this to us, for he both introduces and grants the existence of non-Euclidean geometry as well as of God's justice. He thus creates the equation only to show that it cannot encompass his whole reality. Through the agency of free will Ivan rejects the terms at the top of the equation:

> I have a Euclidean earthly mind, and how could I solve problems that are not of this world? . . . I believe like a child that all suffering will be healed and made up for . . . [and] at the moment of eternal harmony, something so precious will come to pass that it will suffice for all hearts. . . . but though all that may come to pass, I don't accept it. I won't accept it. Even if parallel lines do meet and I see it myself, I shall see it and say that they've met, but still I won't accept it. (*BK*, 217)

Ivan's language of negation sounds strikingly like Dostoevsky's language of affirmation so many years earlier when, as a convict, he wrote to Madame Fonvizina. Dostoevsky had then affirmed that his love for Jesus was even greater than his love for truth. Ivan divides his universe into two camps as well: like Dostoevsky he maintains that something is more valuable to him than truth; but it is not Jesus, it is his own right not to accept that truth.

It is difficult not to be swayed by Ivan's mighty refusal. Yet Dostoevsky's strategy, both as a political polemicist and as a novelist, typically was to seem to concede everything to his opponent, then, rapidly to reappropriate precisely what had been relinquished. Dostoevsky had already admitted, however, in his letter to Lyubimov, the irrefutability of Ivan's arguments. Will he then refute them? Ivan, like Mitya, tells Alyosha that he has led up to his confession by talking "stupidly," yet Dostoevsky then closes the chapter by having Ivan, smiling like a gentle child, exclaim, "Perhaps I want to be healed by you" (*BK*, , 217).

Virtually as soon as the reader has made the association between Ivan and a little child desiring to be healed, Ivan launches in on his description of the terrible suffering of children on which he bases his renunciation of God's world. Adults, he explains, may have eaten of the apple and may seek retribution, but children, though they are innocent and powerless, still suffer. "If they, too, suffer horribly on earth, they must suffer for their fathers. . . . but that reasoning is of the other world and is incomprehensible for the heart of men here on earth" (*BK*, 219). Moreover, we have just seen a child, Ilyusha, suffer terribly for the sins of his father. It is against this painful and immediate backdrop that the reader experiences Ivan's heartrending enumeration of the sufferings of children.

It is also important to look closely at the unit of agony Ivan describes. Although it is customary and correct to emphasize Ivan's horror at the sufferings of children, in all of his examples *parents* are involved as well—as emblems of infinite love, as tormentors, or perhaps as both. Certainly Ilyusha's father has, against his will, played both roles, as have such characters as Marmeladov in *Crime and Punishment*. If this novel is, as it purports to be, about seeds, about love, and about that great ocean of being that Zosima will shortly describe, all of these elements can take as their fundamental unit the parent-child relationship. Certainly it is this relationship—as opposed to a single figure—that governs the basic lines of the plot. The primary unit of interest for Dostoevsky always involves characters in relationship to others—victim and victimizer, sufferer and healer, confesser and confessor—or in dialogue with themselves.

In addition to this novelistic backdrop, there is Ivan's (and Dostoevsky's) collection of newspaper articles that provides the examples he enumerates. There is a biblical backdrop as well: the Book of Job. Job, too, lost his children as part of his testing as a faithful participant in God's larger truth or design. But Ivan rejects such participation. "And if the suffering of children goes to swell the sum of sufferings which was necessary to pay for truth, then I protest that the truth is not worth such a price. I don't want the mother to embrace the oppressor who threw her son to the dogs! She dare not forgive him! Let her forgive him for herself . . . but the sufferings of her tortured child she has no right to forgive. . . . I would rather remain with my unavenged suffering and unsatisfied indignation, *even if I were wrong*" (*BK*, 226). Ivan, like Dostoevsky, puts the passion of his being into a vessel that is somehow beyond truth. For the Dostoevsky who wrote to Madame Fonvizina, this valuing of something that is beyond Truth eventually led him to a miraculous affirmation of life, whereas, temporarily at any rate, Dostoevsky gives Ivan this same phraseology to enable him to negate life.

We see yet another example here of the precious grain of his own experience that he was willing to give up to the transforming power of art. Ivan at last utters his famous words, "And so I hasten to give back my entrance ticket." We may have thought Smerdyakov a scoundrel when he expressed the same idea (*BK*, 206), but coming from Ivan these words do not fail to move. Ivan then goes on to state the proposition that had haunted Dostoevsky ever since he first read Balzac's *Père Goriot* (1834) as a young man, and that informed the genesis of *Crime and Punishment*. Ivan puts the vital proposition before Alyosha: "Imagine that you are creating a fabric of human destiny with the object of making men happy in the end, giving them peace and rest at last, but that it was essential and inevitable to torture to death only one tiny creature—that little child beating its breast with its fist, for instance—and so found that edifice on its unavenged tears, would you consent to be the architect on those conditions? Tell me and tell the truth" (*BK*, 225). We have become accustomed, lulled as readers throughout the novel, to Dostoevsky's method, and his narrator-chronicler's, of presenting parodies or comic statements of important ideas before their serious presentation. Yet here a new mode comes subtly into play. Ivan, before he even begins his poem of the Grand Inquisitor, has put forth its central question, the fundamental riddle about human experience with which this novel is asking its readers to grapple.

Let me digress for a moment to that key passage in *Père Goriot*. Keep in mind, however, that Ivan is consciously "confessing" to Alyosha and that Dostoevsky himself had an extremely ambivalent view of the possibility that an authentic confession could take place between one speaker and one listener, particularly when any prepared text was involved. Indeed, much of his fiction can be read as a veiled polemic with that archetypal master of the confessional genre, Jean-Jacques Rousseau, author of *Confessions* (1781). Thus, when we turn to *Père Goriot* and the original statement of that proposition that had for so long haunted Dostoevsky, it is no surprise to find Rousseau lurking behind it all. Rastignac and Bianchon are conversing in the Luxembourg Gardens.

"You may laugh, but you don't know what you're laughing at. Have you read Rousseau?"

"Yes."

"Do you remember the passage where he asks the reader what he would do if he could make a fortune by killing an old mandarin in China by simply exerting his will, without stirring from Paris?"

"Yes."

"Well?"

"Bah! I'm at my thirty-third mandarin."

"Don't play the fool. Look here, if it were proved to you that the thing was possible and you only needed to nod your head, would you do it?"

"Is your mandarin well-stricken in years? But, bless you, young or old, paralytic or healthy, upon my word—the devil take it! Well, no."[4]

Throughout this dialogue Rastignac's role prefigures Ivan's, and Balzac's Bianchon resembles Alyosha.

This Balzacian conversation, with its roots in Rousseau, has profound resonances in *The Brothers Karamazov,* where Ivan takes the economic-moral proposition set forth by Rousseau and Balzac and transforms it into a metaphysical-moral one. It no longer concerns just one man's prosperity but has become a symbol for the entire human edifice.

It is typical of Dostoevsky as a borrower and adapter to use several sources at once, including, most often, himself—either his experience or his own past work. Here we find a biblical source (the Book of Job), two literary ones (Rousseau's *Confessions* and Balzac's *Père Goriot*), traces of *Crime and Punishment* and *The Idiot,* and finally, a response to the recent death, for which he felt responsible, of his own child. But only here at the end of his career does Dostoevsky succinctly and absolutely, through the words of Ivan—"would you consent to be the architect on those conditions?"—ask the question that had haunted him for his whole adult life.

By the time Ivan prepares to recite his poem in prose—composed a year earlier but never written down—the reader may wonder what more could possibly come? How can this pitch and fervor be sustained? How can the substance of the poem compete with the prelude to it? It is no wonder that critic after critic has found in these chapters some of the most powerful prose ever written.

What does the chapter title, "Rebellion," signify? Who in fact has rebelled, Ivan or Alyosha? Ivan describes to the angelic Alyosha the conflicting processes of affirmation and renunciation he has already struggled with, but in the very act of telling he precipitates a similar reaction in Alyosha. Before meeting Ivan at the tavern, Alyosha had merely been depressed; now he finds that he accepts, at least in part, the ramifications of Ivan's metaphysical equation. Ivan describes the sadistic general whose dogs devour the child before his mother's eyes: " 'Well, what did he deserve? To be shot? To be shot for the satisfaction of our moral feelings? Speak, Alyoshka!' 'To be shot,' murmured Alyosha, lifting his eyes to Ivan with a pale, twisted smile" (*BK,* 224).

A few minutes later Alyosha recovers himself and reaffirms the idea of Christ as that being who can forgive everything, "because He gave His innocent blood for all. . . . You have forgotten Him, and on Him is built the edifice" (*BK*, 227). But Alyosha's recovery of his faith cannot undo its momentary loss. It is Alyosha's words about Jesus that remind Ivan of his poem in prose. "You will be my first reader—that is, listener. Why should an author forego even one listener?" (*BK*, 227). By the close of the chapter it becomes oddly difficult to say who is healing whom, who is in crisis, who is rebelling.

Ivan begins his poem of the Grand Inquisitor with a literary preface that shows off his knowledge and functions well within the medieval scholastic tradition of citing numerous sources and models to prepare the way for one's "own word." It is typical of both Dostoevsky and his literary creation, Ivan, that the scholastic habit of citing sources becomes an excuse to concoct a hearty stew containing some unexpected ingredients. Dante, French clerks and monks, the religious plays performed in the court of Peter the Great, Russian monks—all are more or less likely sources for this historical tale. But then we find a contemporary source in Victor Hugo's *Nôtre Dame de Paris* and his rendition of "Le bon jugement de la très sainte et gracieuse Vierge Marie." This recalls to Ivan's mind another important source about the Virgin Mary, "The Wanderings of Our Lady through Hell," a twelfth-century apocryphal tale. Suddenly the roles reverse: we have the specter of a mother who does plead for mercy to be shown "all without distinction." And God here, in Ivan's rendition, echoes Ivan's rebellious words of a few moments earlier. He "points to the hands and feet of her Son, nailed to the Cross, and asks, 'How can I forgive His tormentors?' " (*BK*, 228). But Mary prevails. Under her influence God offers up a kind of limited or conditional forgiveness. Thus Ivan offers a paradoxical counterpoint to his own just uttered words: "Let her forgive the torturer for the immeasurable suffering of her mother's heart. But the sufferings of her tortured child she has no right to forgive; she dare not forgive the torturer, even if the child were to forgive him" (*BK*, 226). In Ivan's rendering of this apocryphal tale, God has, in part, agreed with Ivan, but Mary has gone ahead with her own forgiveness. Ivan's most powerful interlocutor is his own literary sensibility.

Most important, Ivan's preface continues the dominant thematic motifs that have governed all of Book V: the interconnected problems of parent-child (shepherd and flock) relations and suffering—both the imposition and the endurance of it. Ironically, the poem, the most powerful statement of Ivan's rebellion, begins with a preface whose main episode has been about forgiveness. What is even more surprising perhaps is that forgiveness will figure at the close of Ivan's poem as well. Thus, as readers, we would do well to ask ourselves, what is the relationship of the opening and closing frames to the poem itself?

After his preface Ivan offers up a one-sentence summary of his poem: "He comes on the scene in my poem, but He says nothing, only appears and passes on" (*BK,* 228). Key, then, are His arrival, His departure, His silence. According to Ivan's tale, Jesus appears in Seville during the time of the Spanish Inquisition. "He came softly, unobserved, and yet, strange to say, everyone recognized him. That might be one of the best passages in the poem" (*BK,* 229).

Ivan's ongoing literary critique of his own poem as he narrates it to Alyosha sets up a complex interplay, which continues through the rest of this pivotal chapter, between Alyosha as listener (audience) and sometime critic and Ivan as author and sometime critic as well. This interplay becomes even more complex as the reader begins to discern the similarities between Ivan and his Grand Inquisitor and between Alyosha and Jesus. The net result is a blurring of the usual lines of demarcation between subject and object, author and subject, author and critic, author and audience, and audience and subject. Most significant for the model of reading imposed in this novel by Dostoevsky, this crucial blurring may extend even to the boundary between character and reader.

Moreover, given the growing preoccupation in the novel, and particularly in Ivan's recent words, with children, it is fitting that Jesus' single act on arriving in Seville is to raise a child from the dead. There is a mother's joy, as well as general weeping, cries, and confusion, at the enactment of this miracle. Ivan's words in the previous two chapters have prepared us to rejoice at this miracle, for he, Alyosha, and we with them have just heartily rejected any edifice, however just, built on the tears of even a single child.

Yet Jesus' miracle still looms as problematic—mysterious—for he has here chosen to save a single child but not any of those "hundred heretics" burned at the stake the day before. Is Ivan indirectly testing his own proposition? Our emotions at this point are operating in a reverse manner from the way in which Ivan structured his argument. Just moments earlier Ivan had argued that he would not even concentrate on adults, who have already eaten of the apple, but would instead focus on children. Yet surely in this chapter we *do* find ourselves more engaged with the vivid agonies of the nameless multitude (those dirty sinners who have already eaten of the apple) than we *do* with the possible suffering endured by the little girl, resting in her coffin of flowers, whom Jesus raises? This refocusing of emotional energy is paradoxical; it also underscores the axiom in this novel that miracles, when they do occur, are mysterious, unheralded events that do not serve to solve general problems.

Jesus arrives on this dreadful scene of religious massacre, but he solves no problems and does not alleviate the intense sufferings of the people. He saves a single child, not even a beggar child but the daughter of a prominent citizen, a child who had died a natural death. It almost seems a pointless miracle, given the terrible, unjustified sufferings of the dying multitudes. But it is not, for as we shall see, it reflects the ongoing determination of Jesus not to give in, in any way, to those three temptations proposed to him by the devil in the wilderness some 15 centuries earlier.

The Grand Inquisitor comes on the scene, exercises his firm authority over the people, and has Jesus arrested. Late that night he visits Jesus in his cell and "speaks openly of what he has thought in silence for ninety years" (*BK,* 231). A tension begins to emerge between words and silence: the Grand Inquisitor speaks, Jesus is silent; Ivan speaks, Alyosha, for the most part, listens in silence. According to the Grand Inquisitor, the most "stupendous miracle" of all had involved the statement of words and had occurred on the day that "the great spirit talked with Thee in the wilderness. . . . The statement of those three questions was itself the miracle. . . . From those questions alone, from the miracle of their statement, we can see that we have here to do not with the fleeting human intellect, but with the absolute and the eternal. For in those three questions the whole subsequent history of mankind is, as it were, brought together into one whole, and foretold, and in them are united all the unsolved historical contradictions of human nature" (*BK,* 232–33).

The Grand Inquisitor, the devil, and perhaps Ivan—because it is he who gives the Grand Inquisitor these words—believe that these statements constitute a miracle because they encapsulate and predict the contradictions and the shape of human history. Jesus, God, Alyosha, and, as we shall see, Zosima indicate indirectly that the miracle lies elsewhere. But words remain crucial to it—perhaps the words with which Jesus answers the devil. But where does that leave silence?

Silence becomes part of the mystery, part of the measure of man's freedom of choice, a verbal absence somehow related to that moment when the seed (word) dies and before it brings forth its great fruit. Dostoevsky frequently offers up to us for consideration rich polarities and juxtapositions, but they never operate in a mechanistically binary way. Words are instruments of both God (grace) and the devil (damnation); silence may be a force of divine good (Jesus' silence here) or may work toward the enabling of evil. (Ivan's later moments of silence are a dangerous goad, an acquiescence.)

The Grand Inquisitor then proceeds to restate the events described in the New Testament, especially in the gospels of Matthew and John, in which the devil appears to Jesus and sets before him the three temptations. The devil urges Jesus to turn stones into bread. "Turn them into bread, and mankind will run after Thee like a flock. . . . But Thou wouldst not deprive man of freedom and didst reject the offer, thinking what is that freedom worth, if obedience is bought with bread? Thou didst reply that man lives not by bread alone" (*BK*, 233). The Grand Inquisitor then goes on to make an argument that continues to exert tremendous force on the social and ethical thought of our time: "Feed men, and then ask of them virtue!" The Grand Inquisitor argues that he and his church, by caring for the weak and by lying to them—saying, "We are Thy servants and rule . . . in Thy name"—are showing greater love for mankind than Jesus. "That deception will be our suffering. . . . Didst Thou forget," asks the Grand Inquisitor, "that man prefers peace, and even death, to freedom of choice in the knowledge of good and evil?" (*BK*, 235). Earlier the Grand Inquisitor had asked, "Dost Thou know that the ages will pass, and humanity will proclaim by the lips of their sages that there is no crime, and therefore no sin; there is only hunger?" (*BK*, 233).[5] The Grand Inquisitor repeats the rationale that virtually every totalitarian system has used to justify its rule, but he also, paradoxically, repeats the beliefs of many benevolent social thinkers and philanthropists.

It is well known that Dostoevsky struggled in all his novels against the prevailing liberal notion of his day, and our own, that criminal acts can be explained away, even excused, by the terrible effect on the criminal of an environment of suffering and poverty. Yet this is not to say that Dostoevsky opposed alleviating dreadful conditions. His letters and, above all, his *Diary of a Writer* reflect his compassion and his understanding of precisely such potentially adverse effects of environment. Nevertheless, he believed that the capacity to choose between good and evil was present in every human being and should be exercised everywhere.

Moreover, the Grand Inquisitor deftly twists the import of Jesus' response to this first temptation by failing to quote it fully. "It is written, Man shall not live by bread alone, but by every word that proceedeth out of the mouth of God" (Matt. 4:4). The full utterance carries a different connotation, an acknowledgment that bread is indeed important, but the words of God are more so. The Grand Inquisitor's silence about the second part of Jesus' answer returns us to that tension between words and silence. The devil, as Fyodor had observed in Part I, is the father of lies, of words twisted and misshapen. Here the Grand Inquisitor reflects his allegiance to the devil by presenting Jesus' own words to Him, and to us, in misshapen, elliptical form.

The Grand Inquisitor then asserts that there are only three powers that can hold captive the consciences of men and make them happy: miracle, mystery, and authority. "We have corrected Thy work and founded it upon miracle, mystery, and authority" (BK, 237). He accuses Jesus of having rejected all three. In Ivan's poem the Grand Inquisitor will repeat these three words until they gain an incantatory force and become lodged in the reader's mind. At the center of his novel, in the "deep heart's core" occupied jointly by the Grand Inquisitor's words, as spoken by Ivan, and by Zosima's words, as transcribed and edited by Alyosha, Dostoevsky states the key ideas of his novel in their most naked, unadorned, vulnerable form. The riddles of miracle, mystery, and authority figure at the heart of both the Grand Inquisitor's diatribe and Zosima's exhortations, and each uses the rhetoric of persuasion to the utmost. The rest of the novel will renew and recast their words.

In the second temptation, which we have already seen extensively parodied through Smerdyakov's verbal antics, the devil tries to persuade Jesus to hurl himself from the pinnacle of the Temple to show His faith that God would not let Him fall. "Thou didst know then that in taking one step . . . Thou wouldst be tempting God and have lost all Thy faith in Him" (BK, 236). But the Grand Inquisitor argues that men, unlike Jesus, need miracles "at the great moments of their life, the moments of their deepest, most agonizing spiritual difficulties" (BK, 236).

And indeed, the force of the Grand Inquisitor's words will shortly be borne out in Alyosha's own spiritual crisis, whose beginnings are already so evident. He will experience that wrenching need for a miracle at his moment of spiritual difficulty, and it will not come. Like the miracle performed by Jesus at the beginning of Ivan's poem, the miracle that does come—if any does—will be oddly gratuitous and will occur only after Alyosha has clung, simply and devotedly, "to the free verdict of the heart."

As Ivan's narrative continues, the doubling between him and his Inquisitor and between Alyosha and Jesus grows more intense. As the Grand Inquisitor says to Jesus, "And why dost Thou look silently and searchingly at me with Thy mild eyes?" it is the image of Alyosha sitting silently before Ivan that comes to mind. It is at this moment that the Grand Inquisitor lays bare his mystery (and Dostoevsky lays bare his ultimate condemnation of the Church of Rome): "We are not working with Thee, but with *him*—that is our mystery" (*BK*, 238).

The Grand Inquisitor reveals that the Church had also accepted the devil's third temptation, "that last gift." "We took from him Rome and the sword of Caesar, and proclaimed ourselves sole rulers of the earth" (*BK*, 238). Here Dostoevsky welds together his dislike of the Catholic Church and socialist thought, which he believed were both moving toward atheism and the enslavement of man. He has the Grand Inquisitor spout the language of nineteenth-century socialism tempered with Dostoevsky's own journalistic language of political polemic: "We shall plan the universal happiness of man"; we shall find a means of "uniting all in one unanimous and harmonious anthill" (*BK*, 238). The ambiguity of Ivan's article, which the monks had argued about in Part I, now becomes clearer. The Church that becomes the State has, quite simply, succumbed to the temptation of the devil.

Having gone through his explanatory argument, the acceptance of the three temptations, and the incantatory evocations of miracle, mystery, and authority, the Grand Inquisitor's self-justificatory statement takes a new, poignant, yet familiar twist that brings the novel back to its own reality—the impending spiritual crises of the three brothers, and the overarching theme of parents and children. The Grand Inquisitor accuses Jesus of being a poor shepherd to His flock, a poor father to His children. He claims for himself and his church true compassion for humanity. They "will look to us and huddle close to us in fear, as chicks to the hen. . . . Oh, we shall allow them even sin. They are weak and helpless, and they shall love us like children because we allow them sin . . . and the punishment for these sins we take upon ourselves" (*BK*, 240). Are the Grand Inquisitor's compassion and love counterfeit or genuine?

He argues that he will stand at the judgment day before God and justify his lies in the name of "the thousands of millions of happy children who have known no sin" (*BK*, 240). Has the Grand Inquisitor constructed an edifice that is *not* founded on the unexpiated tears of a child? At this moment of the Grand Inquisitor's moving verbal crescendo we may be tempted to believe that he has. Dostoevsky has, once again, duplicated in the experience of reading the philosophical and metaphysical problems with which his novel abounds: he tempts us.

The narrator-chronicler tells us that Alyosha listens in silence, though toward the end he becomes greatly moved and is on the point of interrupting. Do these words also describe Jesus as He listened to the Grand Inquisitor? At any rate, Alyosha's response may come as a surprise: "Your poem is in praise of Jesus, not in blame of Him—as you meant it to be" (*BK*, 241). Has the Grand Inquisitor indirectly defeated his own argument, and has Jesus' silence ultimately been even more rhetorically persuasive than the Grand Inquisitor's words?

Alyosha at last asks Ivan how the poem ends. "Or was it the end?" Ivan replies that the silent Prisoner looked the Grand Inquisitor quietly and gently in the face. Then suddenly "He approached the old man in silence and softly kissed him on his bloodless aged lips. That was all his answer. The old man shuddered. His lips moved." He goes to the door and lets Him go. " 'And the old man?' 'The kiss glows in his heart, but the old man adheres to his idea' " (*BK*, 243). A few moments later Alyosha duplicates this kiss, even as the narrator-chronicler echoes Ivan's words: "Alyosha got up, went to him and softly kissed him on the lips." Ivan, ever the author-critic, exclaims, though with delight, "That's plagiarism . . . You stole that from my poem" (*BK*, 244). Ivan is right, of course; we have just witnessed an example of the most fundamental power of literature (the word): it offers up an artistic model that can inspire one in life. Art may imitate life, but as Oscar Wilde's famous aphorism affirms, life imitates art. This is not Alyosha's first act of plagiarism, however; nor will it be his last.

Indeed, Alyosha's greatest gift as a "good man" in his ability to give back to others what they have given him—what they, unknowingly, already possess. At this moment, Alyosha may, through his loving kiss, be sowing in Ivan the seed of his own redemption. But that kiss actually originates in Ivan's sensibility; it is he who has created the parable of a Jesus who kissed the old sinner; it is he who describes how the kiss glowed in the old atheist's heart. We may ask again what we asked at the outset of Book V: who is saving whom? The chapter closes with a crescendo of religious symbolism as Ivan departs to the left and Alyosha to the right. Alyosha also notices that "Ivan swayed as he walked and that his right shoulder looked lower than his left" (*BK*, 245; see also *BK, 256, 257*).

The many correspondences of Ivan's confession with Mitya's suddenly strike Alyosha. "The strange resemblance flashed like an arrow through Alyosha's mind." Moreover, the wind again rose, "as on the previous evening, and the ancient pines murmured gloomily" (*BK*, 243). And once again Alyosha hurries back to his monastery, burdened with the sad knowledge that his two brothers, and perhaps he himself, are on the brink of disaster. But even as he takes note of the resemblance between these two confessional episodes, Alyosha forgets that he has not yet found Mitya, the search for whom has until this moment guided his movements.

Book V closes with nightmarish intimations of Ivan's oncoming madness—"Some person or thing seemed to be standing out somewhere, just as something will sometimes intrude itself upon the eye"— and with his dreadful encounter with Smerdyakov. The atmosphere quickly fills with stifling foreboding. Alyosha has departed for the monastery, and the demonic lackey Smerdyakov enacts his temptations. " 'I am a scoundrel,' whispers Ivan to himself" (*BK*, 260).

BOOK VI

Dostoevsky had originally planned for Book VI, "The Russian Monk," to be part of Book V, but while working on it he realized that they could not fit together into a single book (*Letters*, 464–65, 467). Taken together, however, these two books form the core of *The Brothers Karamazov*.

Throughout the rest of the novel, and particularly in "The Russian Monk," Dostoevsky seeks, albeit indirectly, to answer the questions raised by Ivan and the Grand Inquisitor. On 19 May 1879, Dostoevsky wrote to the conservative Konstantin Pobedonostev: "Well, I have finished and mailed off the blasphemy but will send the refutation only for the June issue. . . . The refutation (not a direct one, i.e., not in a face-to-face argument) will come as the last words of the dying elder. Many critics have reproached me for generally choosing, as it were, wrong themes for my novels, themes that are not realistic, etc.; but I feel, on the contrary, that there is nothing more realistic than precisely these themes" (*Letters*, 467). A month later he wrote to Lyubimov: "In the next book there will be the death of Father Zosima and his last conversations with friends. This is not a sermon, but rather a sort of story, an account of an incident in his own life." Dostoevsky then stated what had been an artistic obsession of his since the writing of *The Idiot*—the desire to portray successfully, in an interesting way, a positively good man: "If I can bring it off, I will have accomplished something useful: *I will force them to admit* that a pure and ideal Christian is not an abstraction but a tangible, real possibility that can be contemplated with our own eyes [Dostoevsky's italics]" (*Letters*, 469–70). He then expressed yet another typical concern—his desire to be original, to portray "new types."

Indeed, although Dostoevsky was frequently his own harshest critic and was often ready to admit the failure of a particular work, he was virtually never prepared to give up his claims to originality. His letter to Lyubimov continued: "I pray God that I may succeed. . . . But above all, the theme is one that would never even occur to any other contemporary writer or poet, and so, it is completely *original*. It is for this theme that the entire novel is being written" (*Letters*, 470). Ironically, Dostoevsky neglected to mention that there was indeed another novel written on this theme—his own *The Idiot*.

Dostoevsky himself was the first to criticize "The Russian Monk." Interestingly, he used the very same language (and even the same fraction) he had used over a decade earlier in 1869 to describe the failure of *The Idiot*. Again he stands up for his idea, then laments, "I am not certain, though, that I have done it successfully. I myself feel that I have not been able to express ⅒ of what I would have liked to. Nevertheless, I view this Book Six as the culminating point of the novel."[6] The question is, do we?

In this letter Dostoevsky also expressed what perhaps, after his faith in his own artistic originality, mattered most to him in his conception of himself as an artist: that his characters speak with their own voices, not with his. Bakhtin based his theories of polyphony and multivoicedness—which have so enhanced our thinking about Dostoevsky's literary writings and about the form of the novel in general—on this aspect of Dostoevsky's art, his capacity to create characters who speak with voices that are wholly and indelibly their own.

As early as 1846 Dostoevsky had complained about those readers who confused him with Goldyadkin, the psychotic hero of *The Double* (1846). Later he berated those readers of *Notes from the House of the*

Dead who thought that he, like his narrator, had been sent to prison for the murder of his wife. Thus it is particularly fitting that so close to the end of his life Dostoevsky should have yet again asserted his crucial distance from his literary creation—this time from a character whose beliefs on many subjects did, in fact, coincide with his own. Yet always, for Dostoevsky, the way in which an idea is expressed, the individual personality behind it, was more important than the idea itself, for the idea exists only in each character's individual manifestation of it. Thus idea becomes inseparable from its mode of presentation.

A passage from the same letter in which Dostoevsky wrote of his worries about the success of Book VI illustrates this fundamental artistic and semantic belief: "It goes without saying that many of the teachings of my Elder Zosima (or should I rather say, his way of expressing them) are inherent in his personality, i.e., in the manner in which his character is portrayed. And although I fully share the thoughts he expresses, if I were to express them myself, *in my own voice,* I would do so in another language and in another form." The overriding, paradoxical irony is that when Dostoevsky did do this in his journalism, he often failed to move his readers. But the results of his leap into art, into empathy, into the voice of another, has virtually always moved them. Dostoevsky continued: "But he *could not* express himself in any other language or *in any other spirit* than the one I have ascribed to him. Otherwise, I would have failed to create a live literary character [Dostoevsky's italics]" (*Letters,* 477).

Dostoevsky went on to insist that his chapter divisions and those of his character Alyosha, who has divided up his manuscript about Zosima's teachings "in his own way," be respected. He chided Lyubimov about his printing of *The Grand Inquisitor.* "You not only failed to respect my division, you even had 10 consecutive pages without a *single paragraph break.* This upset me a great deal, and I am lodging a cordial complaint with you [Dostoevsky's italics]" (*Letters,* 478).

A few days before "The Russian Monk" was due to appear Dostoevsky wrote that he was trembling over whether it would adequately answer the negative ideas expressed in *The Grand Inquisitor* (*Letters,* 465, 467–470). Again he affirmed that his refutation was through indirect means. Yet how indirect are his means? How *does* Dostoevsky refute the negative view with a positive one? If his means, as he maintained, are indirect, what is the nature of this indirection? Was he right to have trembled?

We have already seen how Ivan's Grand Inquisitor claimed that the Catholic Church had accepted from the devil the very temptations— whose statement was the "great miracle"—that Jesus had rejected and had drawn its power over people from miracle, mystery, and authority. Ivan had composed his poem a year earlier and had recited it for the first time to Alyosha.

The form that Zosima's last exhortations take is equally unusual. Alyosha, like Ivan, relies on his memory; he writes down Zosima's last conversations and exhortations "some time after his elder's death." The narrator takes pains to show us that this narrative constitutes an intimate superimposition of Alyosha's editorial decisions on Zosima's actual words. "But whether this was only the conversation that took place then, or whether he added to it his notes of parts of former conversations with his teacher, I cannot determine" (*BK*, 265). The narrator-chronicler concludes Book VI with even more disclaimers about Alyosha's principles of composition and his editorial philosophy: "I repeat, it is incomplete and fragmentary" (*BK*, 303). In fact, Dostoevsky is saying to us behind his narrator's back, "I repeat, it is complete, and there is a whole there for the reader to discern." Moreover, Alyosha hands these conversations down to us as a monologue, in a genre that Dostoevsky's readers would know well, a "saint's life": *Notes of the Life in God of the Deceased Priest and Monk, the Elder Zosima, Taken from his Own Words by Alexey Fyodorovich Karamazov.*

Thus the document the reader encounters is itself a product of indirection, of multiple layers of mediation. Zosima's words are refracted through the prism of Alyosha, who reports them for his own reasons. The narrator-chronicler frames them with his own observations, and, of course, the author Dostoevsky orchestrates all these voices at once. Thus this single document, which contributes to what Bakhtin would call the polyphony of voices in the novel, is *itself* composed of polyphonic units. The smallest phrase from Zosima's *Life* is a polyphonic one, containing at all times the traces of Zosima, Alyosha, the narrator-chronicler, and the author. Book VI, despite its seeming simplicity of design and serenity of event, is the most complex narrative in the novel.

Moreover, this complexity of form, which is, so to speak, encased in an envelope of uniformity (Zosima's life), becomes a kind of metaphor-through-text of the novel's epigraph from John 12:24 about the seed. Indeed, it is here that the epigraph takes its first strong root in the novel and becomes indelibly linked to the theme of memory. Yet this theme of memory takes us back full circle to the question of the narrative texture of Book VI, whose message from Zosima, composed literally out of his memories of his life, is mediated through the later memories—recollections in tranquillity—of Alyosha.

The framework of Ivan's rebellion is his horror at the unjustified suffering of children and his refusal to participate in a non-Euclidean geometry of forgiveness. Zosima takes a similar starting point. He tells us that, as a child of eight, he "consciously received the seed of God's word in my heart" (*BK*, 270) through reading in church the Book of Job.[7] (We also learn that he had read it again "yesterday" with tears, that is, he read it on the day that the peasant woman whose child had died came to him.) Zosima's rendering of the story of Job has brought upon Dostoevsky the charge of subscribing, at least in part—or when it suits his purposes as an artist—to the Manichean heresy, for here in the words Zosima uses to paraphrase the Book of Job the devil seems to be successful in tempting God to action, much in the same way that he later fails in the desert to tempt Jesus. Zosima's account, mediated through Alyosha's pen, continues in a vein that implies God and the devil are engaged in an open-ended contest: "And God boasted to the devil, pointing to his great and holy servant. And the devil laughed at God's words. 'Give him over to me and Thou wilt see that Thy servant will murmur against Thee and curse Thy name.' And God gave up the just man He loved so, to the devil. And the devil smote his children" (*BK*, 270).

It is in this terrible story (the words almost sound like Ivan's) of the unjust suffering of Job's children that Zosima discovers the true mystery of Christian faith. He finds himself able to accept precisely that mystery, that non-Euclidean geometry, which Ivan so passionately rejects. "Many years pass by, and he has other children and loves them. But how could he love those new ones when those first children were no more, when he has lost them? Remembering them, how could he be fully happy with those new ones, however dear the new ones might be? But he could, he could. It's the great mystery of human life that old grief passes gradually into quiet tender joy" (*BK*, 271). Zosima does not counter Ivan's argument through reason or logic, but through the heart, through the emotional repetition, "he could, he could." He gives himself up to an acceptance of what he experiences as a true mystery. Mystery remains a mystery; faith is an unfathomable giving up of oneself, an acceptance of mystery.

Ivan's Grand Inquisitor claims to take authority upon himself, to

assume responsibility before God for men in exchange for their freedom. Throughout Book VI, Zosima takes pains to disperse authority
among all men, authority takes the form of the personal and equal
responsibility of each person for everyone else—for being one's
brother's keeper. It is a dying child, his brother Markel, who first
impresses this idea upon the 10-year-old Zosima. "Everyone is really
responsible to all men for all men and for everything" (*BK*, 268).
Zosima repeats this idea as a kind of incantation. For him, true authority transfigures and disperses itself into responsibility, a radically egali-
tarian responsibility of each for all and all for each. The Grand Inquisitor's model of authority is vertical, Zosima's horizontal.

Ivan's Grand Inquisitor argues that man should barter away his
freedom in exchange for security, a security brought about by the
Church's hocus-pocus manipulation of miracle, mystery, and authority.
Zosima's narrative does not counter this proposition. Instead, it funda-
mentally revises the structure of the basic argument; it changes the
terms of the equation. Zosima does not see man's freedom as a commodity to be traded away in exchange for security. Rather, it is only when
man is free that he can experience and express his relationship with
God.

Zosima's narrative, taken as a whole, exemplifies miracle, mystery,
and authority in their redeeming rather than their enslaving aspects.
Zosima witnesses the mysterious and miraculous spiritual conversion
of Markel. Later, as a young officer, he strikes his servant Afanasy just
before he is to fight a duel. Suddenly he weeps; he remembers the words
of his dying brother, and a conversion descends on him. His authority
over his servant changes instantaneously into a relationship of mutuality. "I dropped at his feet and bowed my head to the ground. 'Forgive
me,' I said" (*BK*, 277). A moment earlier he had remembered, from so
many years before, Markel's words, "Am I worth it?" and had silently
applied them to himself. Suddenly his servant, who, of course, has no
knowledge of Markel or his words, cries out, "Am I worth it?" and
begins to sob. In this mysterious passing on of the emblematic phrase
"Am I worth it?" through the agency of both memory (the past) and
utterance (the present), we see a literalization of the central metaphor,
the seed, and a specific example of how grace (words as seeds) travels
through the novel.

Markel's words and the words of the Book of Job plant a seed of
grace in the heart of the child Zosima. The seed dies in him; he leads a
life of dissipation. It then brings forth fruit; he experiences a conver-

sion. Meanwhile, he begins, through his words to his servant, to pre-cipitate a conversion within him and later within the mysterious visitor as well.

Alyosha too had received a childhood experience of grace, through the love of his mother. He also listens to these words of Zosima, but to some extent the seed will die in him, too. Yet Alyosha's act of transcrib-ing and rendering Zosima's words shows that he has made them his own, in order to pass them on to those who will read them, including, of course, the readers of the novel. Thus Dostoevsky sought to bring his epigraph to bear on the real world outside the boundaries of his novel and to make his readers participate in this process.

The autobiographical segment of Zosima's narrative has three major parts: the story of his childhood and Markel, and two successive events from his young manhood—the episode with Afanasy and the duel, and his meeting with the mysterious visitor. In his recent book *The Genesis of "The Brothers Karamazov,"* Belknap demonstrates that Zosima first witnesses grace (with Markel), then receives it him-self, and then helps engender or enable it in the mysterious visitor. In the course of the novel Alyosha, Mitya, and Ivan participate in an identical process; moreover, many critics have remarked that these very episodes from Zosima's life resonate in highly specific ways with the lives of the Karamazov brothers.

The young Markel, Zosima tells us repeatedly, resembled Alyo-sha. Zosima even quotes the epigraph as he meditates upon Alyosha's face, and its potential for healing Dmitri's suffering: "I thought your brotherly face would help him. But everything and all our fates are from the Lord. 'Except a corn of wheat fall into the ground and die, it abideth alone; but if it die, it bringeth forth much fruit.' Remember that, Alexey. You, Alexey, I've many times silently blessed you for your face" (*BK*, 264). Zosima goes on to explain that Alyosha's likeness to Markel has been a "reminder" and an "inspiration" to him.

The young Zosima, before his conversion, resembles no one so much as Dmitri. Both men beat a beloved servant and regret it; both are young officers and romantic swashbucklers reminiscent of Push-kin's or Lermontov's heroes. Both struggle with the dictates of two codes of honor that are at variance with each other—a romantic code and an ethical or spiritual one. Both are strikingly good narrators well able to describe psychological details and the ramifications of roads both taken and untaken.

We have already admired Mitya's narrative dexterity in his

confession to Alyosha. Now, as Zosima tells his story to Alyosha, one that chronologically precedes our ongoing plot by decades, he reminds us of Mitya in his predilection for dissecting the layers of motivation that guided his behavior: "I ought to have owned my fault as soon as I got here . . . before leading him into a great and mortal sin; but we have made our life so grotesque, that to act in that way would have been almost impossible, for only after I faced his shot . . . could my words have any significance for him" (*BK*, 278). Zosima's act chronologically prefigures Mitya's, yet Mitya's words in the novel temporally prefigure Zosima's. Alyosha, as the interlocutor of both, stands at the center of this uncanny circle.

Finally, Zosima's mysterious visitor resembles Ivan. Zosima's role in his meetings with his visitor prefigures and echoes Alyosha's vis-à-vis Ivan. The mysterious visitor, like Ivan, tries to live by a theory. Yet his theory does not resemble Ivan's; instead, it bears an unnerving resemblance both to Dostoevsky's own ideas and to the novel's epigraph. The mysterious visitor repeats the assertion that Dostoevsky himself made so often in *Diary of a Writer*: "Paradise . . . lies hidden within all of us" (*BK*, 282). He concretizes and perhaps distorts the message of the epigraph by his theory that we first have to endure a period of isolation, of "terrible individualism," before we will suddenly begin to understand each other (*BK*, 283).

He then confesses to Zosima that he has committed murder. His next words foreshadow Ivan's parable in Book XI about the quadrillion kilometers. The mysterious visitor tells Zosima, "Now I've said it, I feel I've taken the first step and shall go on." Like Ivan and many other Dostoevskian heroes, he makes a public confession that no one believes. Zosima replies by reading John 12:24 (the epigraph of the novel) and Hebrews 10:31. The mysterious visitor assents bitterly to the power of these words: "It's terrible the things you find in these books. . . . Can [these words] have been written by men?" he asks. Zosima, in his role as God's instrument, answers that the Holy Spirit wrote them (*BK*, 288).

Likewise, Alyosha will appear as God's messenger to Ivan in a similarly pivotal scene. "God has sent me to tell you so" (*BK*, 570). The mysterious visitor at last can state, in words that recall Mitya's and Dostoevsky's own attraction to the Manichean heresy, "The Lord vanquished the devil in my heart" (*BK*, 291). Ivan will shortly find himself engaged in an identical battle.

Thus Zosima's narrative offers an indirect answer to Ivan's *Leg-*

end of the Grand Inquisitor. It also represents the fullest working out so far of the epigraph and the myriad interconnecting strands among the themes of grace, seeds, and words. Zosima, like the young Dostoevsky in some of his earliest journalism, passionately advocates reading for the peasants. Words literally become seeds of grace. "Only a little tiny seed is needed—drop it into the heart of the peasant, and it won't die. . . . it will be hidden . . . in the midst of the foulness of his sin, like a bright spot" (*BK*, 272–73). Finally, Zosima's narrative of the past resonates with the same potentials and dilemmas that torment each of the brothers in the novel's present. It recombines them. Taken as a whole, Zosima's narrative is itself a seed, a word, a "bright spot," a "great reminder," and another of those "terrible things" you find in books.

As Book VI closes, the epigraph surges in with a final figurative and literal manifestation. Zosima offers these words of general consolation, "If all men abandon you . . . then when you are left alone fall on the earth and kiss it, water it with your tears and it will bring forth fruit even though no one has seen or heard you in your solitude" (*BK*, 300). Precious memories and tears coalesce, often with the slanting rays of the sun and the sounds of birds, to form a vital bedrock, a moment when a human being is particularly susceptible to the influence of God. The result can be a visionary faith. Zosima concretizes his figure of speech through his own death, as we shall see most fully in Book VII. The actual moment of his death constitutes a triple response of love and recapitulates, with resounding simultaneity, or polyphony, three gestures that we have already seen repeatedly: a bow to the ground, a prayer, and a kissing of the earth.

6

The Plot Quickens
PART III: BOOKS VII, VIII, AND IX

With Part III, Book VII, the second half of the novel commences. From here on the present takes precedence over the past. The history of the Karamazov family, Ivan's poem about the Grand Inquisitor, and the life and thoughts of Zosima have prepared an extraordinarily elaborate structure. The reader can now respond to the rapidly ensuing events of the plot. Indeed, it is plot which dominates the second half of the novel. We read the events of the second half in the language learned in the first: the mythologies explicated in Parts I and II will necessarily order our response to Parts III and IV.

Book VII

In Book VII, "Alyosha," we can read Alyosha's and Grushenka's actions as a demonstration of Zosima's most cherished precepts—John 12:24, his belief about mutual responsibility, his love of falling to the earth and watering it with his tears. Dostoevsky had originally planned to entitle this book "Grushenka," and these two characters do indeed share a valid claim to the title.

The end of Book VI and the beginning of Book VII constitute the dead center of the novel; each is, in fact, full of death. The seed has died; Zosima has fallen to the ground, and his body, contrary to the general expectation and demand for a miracle, has begun to stink (a word that, among its other connotations, recalls "Stinking Lizaveta," the *yurodivaya*, Smerdyakov's mother). Dostoevsky was insistent with his editor about using this word. "I beg you . . . not to delete anything in this Book [VII]. And there is no reason to: *everything is in order*. There is only one little word (about the dead body): *he stank*. But it is said by Father Ferapont, and he can't speak differently." In this letter Dostoevsky also highlights the other key sections of Book VII: "The last chapter . . . *Cana of Galilee* is the most significant in the whole book, perhaps in the whole novel. . . . P.S. . . . I particularly beg you to proofread the legend of the *little onion* carefully. This is a gem, taken down by me from a peasant woman, and of course published for *the first time* [Dostoevsky's italics]."[1]

Upon Zosima's death the townspeople and even Father Paissy succumb to the expectation of an imminent miracle. But no such miracle—to cement and secure faith, as the Grand Inquisitor might say, or as the devil proposed in his second temptation—is forthcoming. Instead, by three o'clock the next day, the narrator-chronicler prudishly and hesitantly reveals, something else has happened: "I may add here, for myself personally, that I feel it almost repulsive to recall that event which caused such frivolous agitation. . . . I would . . . have omitted all mention of it in my story, if it had not exerted a very strong influence on the heart and soul of the chief, though *future*, hero of my story, Alyosha, forming a crisis and turning point in his spiritual development" (*BK*, 308).

This narrative digression is important for several reasons. First, it gives us an important clue to the authorship of the preface to the novel. Upon first reading the novel it is unclear whether we are to assume that the preface at the beginning of the novel is one in which Dostoevsky is directly addressing *his* readers or whether the novel proper has, so to speak, begun and thus it is the narrator-chronicler directly addressing readers in the preface. This digression in Book VII, which is clearly from the perspective of Dostoevsky's created vehicle of the narrator-chronicler, uses a language identical to that of the preface and thus suggests that Dostoevsky intended his preface to be read as a statement by his narrator-chronicler. If so, then we need not assume that Dostoevsky definitely meant to continue his story in future volumes. Second, the narrator-chronicler finds it extremely difficult, unlike Dostoevsky, to mention that the elder "stank." He offers euphemisms—"something," "trivial incident," "that event," "natural and trivial matter." (Behind his back, of course, Dostoevsky is affirming that the seed—in this case, Zosima—must die and "stink" before it can bring forth fruit.) Third, the narrator-chronicler alerts us that this event will be a turning point in Alyosha's life. Alyosha has so far been the recipient of the most important words—seeds—and he has borne witness to Zosima's life, that is, through Zosima he has witnessed grace. The focus will now change. Indeed, at the moment the narrator-chronicler makes his observations Alyosha is "weeping quietly but bitterly" behind a tombstone.

As the criticism in the monastery of Zosima mounts, we hear, among the accusations that he abused the sacrament of confession and that he sat in pride, the angry assertion that he "allowed himself sweet things, ate cherry jam with his tea" (BK, 312). This accusation recalls Alyosha and Ivan in the tavern, when Ivan, parodying the first temptation of Christ, which would form part of his poem a few minutes later, asks, "You don't live by tea alone, I suppose" (BK, 210). And Alyosha's boyhood love of cherry jam turns out to be one of Ivan's most precious memories.

The antics of Father Ferapont in Book VII enact a dark parody of the spiritual truths the novel is attempting indirectly to assert. He claims to cast out Satan even as he brings Satan in. He stands at the head of those who claim to be able to interpret God's meaning in an earthly event. Father Paissy reprimands him four times: for disturbing the peace of the flock, for perhaps serving the evil spirit he claims to be casting out, for claiming to be able to make a judgment that only God can make, and for speaking frivolously. A few minutes later Father Paissy realizes that Alyosha too has begun to expect a miracle, the nonappearance of which has shaken his faith. Alyosha has yielded, however briefly, to the second temptation.

At this point the narrator-chronicler interrupts, proclaiming his own love for Alyosha and asserting that Alyosha is not with those of little faith but with those of great faith. The narrator-chronicler thus inserts his own point of view at this critical moment in his hero's life in much the same way the narrator-chronicler of *The Idiot* does at the critical moment in Myshkin's life. At each of these crucial junctures in the story of the hero—the good man—the language of the narrator-chroniclers is similar to the point of being identical.[2] In Part IV, chapter 9 of *The Idiot*, the narrator-chronicler demurs, "We do not wish at all to justify our hero in the eyes of our readers."[3] "I am far from intending to apologize for him or to justify his innocent faith," says the

Dostoevsky's house in Staraya Russa. Now a museum and gathering place for Dostoevsky scholars

Dostoevsky's study in Staraya Russa in which he worked on *The Brothers Karamazov*

The backyard of Dostoevsky's house: the bathhouse so important to Smerdyakov and his mother, Lizaveta

Staraya Russa. The small local church Dostoevsky attended and where a special mass is said each year at the anniversary of his death

The cathedral by the river in Staraya Russa

A typical street in Skotoprigonevsk (Staraya Russa)

The bridge near which Lizaveta was raped

At left, the store where Mitya bought provisions for Mokroe. At right, the tavern in which Ivan related the *Legend of the Grand Inquisitor* to Alyosha. At center, the square where Mitya pulled Snegiryov's beard and where Kolya teased the peasants.

The back alley and the fence over which Mitya leapt

A "deserted garden"

The swamps and back alleys of Skotoprigonevsk (Staraya Russa)

Grushenka's house—across the river from Dostoevsky's

Boys fishing at the river bank in Staraya Russa

narrator-chronicler about Alyosha as he proceeds to do both. After his justification, he concludes, "Still I am not going to apologize for him" (*BK*, 317). As in *The Idiot*, the more our narrator-chronicler intrudes his presence on the text, the less reliable are his protestations.

The narrator-chronicler defends Alyosha by claiming that he wants not a miracle per se but simply to see higher justice worked out. Thus, if we follow the narrator-chronicler's reasoning, Alyosha longs for a miracle not to secure his faith but simply as a sign of that non-Euclidean justice. And by longing for higher justice in terms he can so readily interpret, Alyosha is really longing for its fulfillment in earthly terms. This thirst for justice links Alyosha, then, to Ivan and strengthens the bond between them. Alyosha, however, longs for the higher justice, while Ivan steadfastly proclaims he will stick to the earthly justice. But God delivers neither justice, as we shall see, on demand.

For all the narrator-chronicler's apologies and justifications, Alyosha has still fallen into error. But the narrator-chronicler counters even this argument: he proclaims that he is prepared to admit that Alyosha's response might have been shallow, but he is still glad his hero unreasonably succumbed to the demands wrought by his love for Zosima. Should we rejoice in Alyosha's fall, since it was caused by love, or should we worry about the demands he has placed on his God?

We learn that as he murmurs against God he experiences an evil impression that stems from his earlier conversation with Ivan. A few moments later Rakitin finds Alyosha face down on the ground, but the earth gives him no sustenance. Rakitin exclaims, with malicious glee, "Do you know, your face is quite changed" (*BK*, 319). Our reading of Book VI has shaped our response to such details, making us more aware of how dire Alyosha's situation is at this moment.

Yet even in his anger and disillusionment Alyosha clings to his faith. "I believe, I believe, I want to believe, and I will believe, what more do you want?" (*BK*, 319). Alyosha expresses his rebellion with another act of plagiarism. Earlier, he had, in imitation of Ivan's Jesus, kissed Ivan. This gesture had given back to Ivan that which was best in him, even though he could not acknowledge it. Now Alyosha mimics Ivan's words to express his turning away from full belief. "I am not rebelling against my God; I simply 'don't accept his world' " (*BK*, 319). Alyosha suddenly smiles a forced smile.

Dostoevsky then gently but firmly piles on the earthly temptations hard and fast. Alyosha accepts sausage meat from Rakitin's pocket, and they set out in search of vodka at Grushenka's house. Rakitin, like the devil in the Book of Job, hopes to bring about the "downfall of the righteous"; he hopes to see Alyosha's fall "from the saints to the sinners" (*BK*, 321). Like Jesus, Alyosha experiences his doubts in a garden, and Rakitin is to be his Judas ready to betray him for 30 pieces of silver.

When Alyosha accompanies Rakitin to Grushenka's, it is no surprise that Grushenka, like so many other characters, confesses to Alyosha. She tells him the story of her seduction and abandonment by the Polish officer who has, at the moment that she is telling her story, already dispatched his messenger to inform her that he awaits her at Mokroe. Her confession reflects the same mix of profoundly contradictory impulses as did those of Dmitri and Ivan. She states that she has forgiven and still loves the officer. Then she admits, "I've grown to love my tears. . . . Perhaps I only love my resentment, not him" (*BK*, 334). Alyosha's gift to her, as with his brothers, is his instinctive response to what is best, most beautiful, and most pure in her words.

Most important, after Grushenka learns that Zosima has died and has "in dismay" slipped quickly off Alyosha's lap, she tells the fable of the onion, which, as noted earlier, Dostoevsky was so pleased to be inserting into his novel. This story, coming as it does at the beginning of the second half of the novel, assumes a vital symbolic weight, comparable to what we have already seen with words, seeds, and bows. All are connected with memory, grace, and love. At the "needed moment," as Zosima would have put it, Grushenka brings forth a "precious memory": she tells Alyosha a story from her childhood about a wicked old peasant woman who had, in the course of her long life, committed only one good deed—she had once given away an onion. Yet the one deed, like a seed long dead, nevertheless embodies the potential of bearing fruit. It could be enough to save her.

The fable's beginning, with the description of the lake of fire in hell, recalls the opening of Ivan's poem in which he cites the apocryphal text of Mary's wanderings through hell. Ivan had also twice referred to Dante's *Inferno*. The hell of Grushenka's folktale also suggests a Dantesque vision of hell; it is full of sinners whose sinfulness continues in hell. Both Mary in Ivan's poem and the old peasant woman's guardian angel in Grushenka's fable manage to prevail upon God to alter his dread sentence. In Ivan's story the sinners had received respite from suffering once a year from Good Friday to Trinity Day. Here, in Grushenka's fable God literally gives the old peasant woman a second chance: she can hold on to the onion and be pulled out of the lake, unless the onion breaks.

Grushenka's fable is in fact a parabolic gloss on Zosima's often repeated aphorism that all are responsible for all. Had the old peasant woman not kicked away the other sinners who were clinging to her in the hope of also being saved, she and all the rest—in a living great chain of being—would have been saved. The sinner in the story is undone and redamned because she cries out, "It's my onion, not yours." But in this chapter Grushenka and Alyosha do the opposite: they cling to each other, and each offers the other an onion; each will hold on to the proffered onion and scramble out of the burning lake (which has often been described, in Alyosha's case, as his furnace of doubt).

This onion, whose meaning has such thematic import, also suggests a metaphor for understanding the structure of the novel. Such terms as "polyphony" and "palimpsest" also offer us ways of apprehending the totality of the narrative. But this simple little garden onion gives the most provocative and heartiest suggestion of all. We have seen the image of seeds dying and bearing fruit, and we have heard each of the major characters speaking in his or her own voice to create a polyphonic effect. The novel, moreover, is certainly a palimpsest with its several cohesive layers of meaning that can exist, if one wishes, independently of each other: a crime novel superimposed on a psychological novel, superimposed on a family novel, superimposed on a metaphysical novel, and so forth.

An onion, like a seed, is a living organism, and to peel away the layers of an onion is to proceed with direction toward a center. Yet each onion layer, the boundaries of which constitute concentric unities in themselves, consists of the same elements as its center. Thus an onion is simultaneously a single entity and a combination of many discrete, layered parts. A slice along its diameter shows its carefully structured and separate layers; to unravel it is to discover that each layer recapitulates all the others. *The Brothers Karamazov* embodies these attributes of the onion. We can admire its narrative layers—from author, to narrator-chronicler, to character, to inserted narratives—but when we pull out any one layer for closer scrutiny, we see that it is contiguous with others and that taken together they form a whole. Where are the boundaries between Ivan, his Grand Inquisitor, his Jesus, and Aloysha, or between Alyosha, Zosima, Markel, the mysterious visitor, and Grushenka? Or between any of the countless combinations of characters we can make? Zosima's love of Markel's face informs his love of

Alyosha's face. When Grushenka finds herself haunted by Alyosha's face (*BK*, 331), she unconsciously crosses into Zosima's territory. When she remembers the story of the burning lake in hell, she trespasses on Ivan's terrain. Yet these encroachments, these correspondences—of which there are literally thousands in the novel (and which contribute to the "confined geography" I described earlier)—give the novel its surprising unity, its miraculously operative metonymy.

"All is like an ocean, all is flowing and blending; a touch in one place sets up movement at the other end of the earth" (*BK*, 299). Zosima's exhortation finds concrete expression in the physical texture of the novel. In Book VII this interconnectedness, this "flowing" and "blending," is particularly evident. Grushenka gives Alyosha both an onion ("You've raised my soul from the depths") and a meta-onion (the entire fable of the onion). Yet moments later, as he takes his leave of her, he smiles at her tenderly and exclaims, with tears, "I only gave you an onion, nothing but a tiny little onion" (*BK*, 335). Who has given whom an onion? No wonder Dostoevsky had trouble deciding on the title of Book VII. Or does the successful giving of the onion depend, as it did in the fable, wholly on mutuality, on shared responsibility? The angel holds out the onion to the sinner. No one must let go of it or push anyone else away.

At any rate, when Alyosha says that he has given Grushenka a tiny little onion, he is once again a saintly plagiarist. Jesus' kiss glows in the Grand Inquisitor's heart—a possible seed of his eventual redemption. Alyosha plagiarizes Ivan's own story by kissing him, but his act, as we have seen, merely returns to Ivan what he already possesses. Likewise Alyosha here gives back to Grushenka the onion from the story she has just told to him—but it was hers to begin with. In each case, the potential for salvation lies within the sinner himself; Alyosha may function as a messenger from God, but he is also a canny intermediary between the parts of the self, a kind of spiritual therapist.

There are, moreover, two kinds of currency that frame the opening and the closing of this chapter. Alyosha arrives at Grushenka's lamenting the treasure he has lost; he then discovers a similar treasure in Grushenka. This invaluable treasure contrasts with the vile Rakitin's earning of 25 rubles. Yet Rakitin, perhaps like Ivan's devil later on in Book XI, and perhaps even like Judas, desires evil but ends up in a roundabout way accomplishing good. Rakitin brings Alyosha to Grushenka in the hope of furthering Alyosha's rebellion; instead, Alyosha, through his encounter with her, finds his way back to the monastery and to God. "Go alone, there's your road," mutters Rakitin abruptly (*BK,* 331).

Alyosha enters Zosima's cell to the sound of Father Paissy reading from John 2:1–10. Before the actual epiphany begins for Alyosha, varied sensations, the narrator-chronicler tells us, move in his soul "in a slow, continual rotation" (*BK,* 337). The narrator, who at the beginning of Book VII was distancing himself from his hero by saying he would not apologize for him or justify his actions, now enters the most private recesses of Alyosha's soul and renders for us an intimate stream of consciousness. The pages of this brief but pivotal chapter gather up numberless stands of the novel into a joyous bouquet.

At first, as Alyosha begins to pray, the fragments of thought flashing though his mind recall the final sections of Zosima's exhortations—his observations about prayer, love, and contact with other worlds. The sound of Father Paissy's voice reading from the Bible recalls that moment so long ago when the boy Zosima felt a godly incense enter his soul as he heard the reading from the Book of Job. For the first time Alyosha is able to think directly about the odor emanating from Zosima's corpse. He names it and is no longer humiliated or hurt by this previously dreadful fact. This third part and third day of the novel coalesce with that third day on which the marriage in Cana of Galilee took place. " 'And the third day there was a marriage in Cana of Galilee,' read Father Paissy" (*BK,* 338). Jesus, Alyosha remembers, visited a scene of joy and there performed his first miracle—an unexpected, nearly gratuitous event. The miracle that Alyosha had expected and hoped for had not taken place, yet by the end of this chapter something else has happened. The back alley, the Lake of Gennaseret (the Sea of Galilee, which also recalls the burning lakes), the intercession of Mary with God, the dead man rising from his coffin and comforting the hiding Alyosha, the dead man's telling that he "gave an onion to a beggar"—all these elements of Alyosha's visionary dream recapitulate and recombine events from the previous three days and from the many words that have been spoken to him. They have all taken root.

At the beginning of Book VII a bitter Alyosha lay face downward on the ground. His heart was breaking. Book VII closes with Alyosha's second fall to the earth, yet this time, in a miraculous moment full of rapturous, nearly sensual religious ecstasy, Alyosha embraces and waters the earth with his tears and "longs to kiss it, kiss it all" (*BK,* 340). (In Russian the intimacy of this passage is·far more intense, for the word for earth is feminine, hence the pronoun *she* echoes through the paragraph.)

Yet always in Dostoevsky's work these heightened moments, which tempt the reader into believing that he is witnessing an actual spiritual conversion, disperse and radiate back through the text when one looks closely. That is, for every conversion, there is a pre-conversion and a pre-pre-conversion and so on. The seed and the onion thus offer clues to both the mechanism by which grace travels through the world and the way a conversion comes about in a single character, as well as suggesting a model for the narrative structure of the novel.

Here, even before Alyosha returns to Zosima's cell and listens to the reading of the Gospel, he had heard Grushenka's fable. Was that the crucial moment when he began to reconsolidate his faith? Or did that moment occur before the telling of the fable when a light seemed to dawn in his face and he said in a firm, loud voice that she had raised up his soul? Or did the key moment occur even before Grushenka knew that Zosima was dead, when she was still sitting on Alyosha's lap and Alyosha, smiling gently at her, put down his glass of champagne? This peeling away of the layers of the onion, this unraveling, makes it hard to isolate any single moment in the spiritual development of Dmitri, Ivan, and Alyosha and define it as the crucial one. Once again the words of Xenos Clark about the journey that is completed before it even takes place come to mind.

BOOK VIII

In Book VIII, Mitya's book, the catastrophe that the narrator-chronicler has prepared for and hinted at for several hundred pages finally occurs. The novel gives itself over to plot. Indeed, Dostoevsky was one of the earliest practitioners of the thriller, a founder of the most durable literary genre of all: the murder mystery, which consists, of course, precisely in the narrator's balancing of disclosure, deception, silence, and arbitrary omniscience. Our narrator-chronicler indulges these literary techniques to the hilt in Book VIII.

Just as Dmitri drastically misreads Grushenka's dilemmas—he thinks she is struggling to choose between father and son and fails to perceive that the returning Polish officer has set her crisis in motion—so do we the readers, along with the characters who are to be "the witnesses," drastically misread and misinterpret Mitya's actions. Our narrator-chronicler plays an even more devious game than he did in Book VII, veering between intimacy and remoteness, knowledge and ignorance—feigned or otherwise.

At this point the narrative of Book VIII begins to rhyme with Mitya's confession to Alyosha in Book III. Mitya, as he did in Book III, runs through various scenarios and plans for action. But through it all he seems fated to kill his father. "Up to the last hour he didn't know [what would happen]. That must be said to his credit" (*BK*, 344). The narrator-chronicler seems to be explaining, even defending Mitya's motives for the murder of Fyodor, even as he is in fact giving us crucial evidence to the contrary. Meanwhile, Mitya, in his desperation, begins to *enact* each of these scenarios. He has lost the fine power of discrimination he displayed in plotting out his strategy vis-à-vis Katerina Ivanovna. Then he was giving away money. But the struggle to obtain money pollutes his sensibility: careful discrimination has given way to frenzied action.

We at last learn why Alyosha and Ivan have been unable to find Mitya for two days. At ten o'clock on the second morning of the novel's action he had first approached the old merchant Samsonov, Grushenka's benefactor and former lover. This first scenario, like his initial, though rejected, plan for winning Katerina Ivanovna, embodies a Karamazov idea. In true Karamazov fashion, Mitya tries to persuade Samsonov to deal in IOUs—Mitya's shaky inheritance claims for the village of Chermashnya against "that unnatural monster" Fyodor—in return for 3,000 rubles. This plan duplicates Fyodor Karamazov's commercial dealings with Grushenka, who has been buying Karamazov IOUs as well. Samsonov, in a grotesque parody of Fyodor with Ivan, sends Mitya off to Chermashnya to negotiate about the copse with the peasant Lyagavy (whose real name is Gorstkin). Mitya, unlike Ivan, actually goes there, armed by the spiteful Samsonov with all the wrong information about how to make the deal work. (Gorstkin hates, for example, to be called Lyagavy.) Moreover, during the second night, while Zosima is dying at the monastery, Mitya actually saves Gorstkin from death. (The charcoal fire in Gorstkin's hut was giving off poisonous fumes, and Gorstkin had passed out in a drunken stupor. But for Mitya's quick and persistent attempt to save him, Gorstkin would have perished.) For us, the goodness of Mitya's spontaneous deed overshadows his other follies, though he himself forgets all about it.

The rhyming with Mitya's narrative in Book III continues. Jealousy motivates Mitya's next round of activity. In the scene succeeding his earlier encounter with Katerina Ivanovna, Mitya had, in a gesture loaded with phallic significance, pulled his sword from its scabbard, kissed it, and replaced it. This odd gesture had embodied both his lust and his honorable repression of it. Now in Book VIII he makes another odd gesture of phallic repression. Mitya, a man who would normally be likely to fight a duel when in a jealous rage, instead prepares to pawn his prized brace of dueling pistols for the ridiculously low sum of 10 rubles.

He then rushes to Madame Khokhlakova's with the equally absurd hope that she, in her desire to prevent his marriage to Katerina Ivanovna, would gladly pay him the 3,000 rubles. Again he tries to sell something he does not own—Chermashnya. Madame Khokhlakova responds with the promise of money: "The money is as good as in your pocket, not three thousand, but three million." She too deals in a nonexistent commodity. "I'll make you a present of the *idea* . . . gold mines" (*BK*, 363). Both of them regard the importance of this exchange as a "mathematical certainty."

Dostoevsky, with high relish in the comedy of this scene, actually parodies an act that in two of his previous novels, *Crime and Punishment* and *The Idiot*, constitutes a key moment of profound solemnity—the act by one character of giving a religious necklace to another. But no gesture, in Dostoevsky's canon, is immune to parody. To conclude their ridiculous encounter, Madame Khokhlakova gives Mitya an icon and puts it around his neck.

The scene between them closes with his roaring anger, and like a maddened comic-tragic hero, Mitya beats himself upon the breast, "on the spot," the narrator-chronicler tells us in a stage whisper, "where he had struck himself two days previously, before Alyosha, the last time he had seen him in the dark, on the road" (*BK*, 366). The narrator-chronicler continues for a full paragraph to highlight the significance of "*that spot*" and Mitya's secret. By turning back to chapter 9 of Book III, we see that the secret is a baseness, a dishonor that he bears on his breast, but a dishonor that could be half-retrieved if he chose to do so (*BK*, 143).

Chapter 3 of Book VIII, which had begun with Mitya pawning his pistols, ends with his grabbing from a mortar "a small brass pestle" about six inches long. This abundance of melodramatic phallic symbols with which descriptions of Mitya seem to abound would be comic if they were not at the same time so representative of his struggles, and if he himself were not so unconscious of them. Later, as Mitya looks with repulsion at the loathed face of his rival (his father, staring out the window and searching for Grushenka), he pulls the brass pestle out of his pocket. This fraught, Freudian, Oedipal moment—illuminated by "slanting lamplight"—creates a shocking phallic icon: the young son drawing his pestle from his pocket to do battle with his father. Although he always claimed to reject such psychological probing, Dostoevsky milks this moment for what it is worth. After an ellipsis come the words: " 'God was watching over me then,' Mitya himself said afterwards" (*BK*, 370).

All of Mitya's actions throughout Book VIII are incomplete: he does not achieve even one of his goals. Along the way the narrator-chronicler throws out a great deal of evidence that cuts both ways, evidence that could buttress the belief that Dmitri had murdered his father, or that he did not. Both paradigms—of incomplete action and of evidence that cuts both ways—come to their climax in the chapter, "In the dark," a chapter that is at once a masterful prevarication and a careful account containing vital clues and facts.

Later that night Mitya redeems the pledge on his pistols and rushes off to Mokroe with champagne, the loaded pistols, and a suicide note in his pocket—"I punish myself for my whole life, my whole life I punish" (*BK*, 380). By reminding us that all this is occurring at "perhaps the very hour" when Alyosha fell to the earth, the narrator-chronicler suggests that Mitya's "sudden resolution" will be of equal spiritual significance. Counterbalanced against this possibility, however, is the narrator's technique, which he so often uses in portraying Mitya, of obfuscation through seeming directness. Instead, the structural paradigm of the uncompleted scenario so frequently associated with Mitya holds: Mitya does not, on this fateful night, kill himself with those loaded pistols. He does experience a spiritual conversion as vital as Alyosha's. Moreover, the further the narrator-chronicler proceeds from the actual moment of the crime, the more genuinely direct and reliable his words about Mitya become.

By the moment of Mitya's most profound epiphany the narrator-chronicler has attached himself to Mitya with the same intimacy that he had shared with Alyosha during the Cana of Galilee episode. In this light, Mitya's act of violence, his decision to kill himself, and his "agonizing confession" correspond paradigmatically to Alyosha's far gentler despair after his elder's death. Although taking a woman on your lap and wanting to eat a bit of sausage with vodka are acts hardly in the same league with potential murder, threatened suicide, and frenzied disorientation, both kinds of acts embody a "death of the seed before it can bring forth great fruit."

Mitya's loaded pistols and his recent striking of a beloved servant in the head also recall Zosima just before his fateful duel. Book VIII begins with Mitya contemplating two endings to his torment. The first would be Grushenka suddenly saying, "Take me, I'm yours forever," and then taking her away to the "furthest end of Russia." The second ending he imagined was an awful one—that she would come to an understanding with Fyodor Pavlovich; and that, if she did, he "did not know what would happen then" (*BK*, 344). By the end of Book VIII these two mutually exclusive outcomes have, in a curious way, come together. Throughout most of Book VIII Mitya acts under the assumption that the second ending will occur, only to discover that the first has happened. The result for the reader, as in Mitya's account of his first encounter with Katerina Ivanovna, is a kind of plot smorgasbord: she can respond to both what does happen and what only seems to happen. The shimmer of the imagined shades the contours of actuality. And as with Alyosha, the actual moment of Mitya's conversion is impossible to isolate.

BOOK IX

Book IX opens with a comic rehashing of recent events. At eleven o'clock in the evening, the young official Perkhotin rushes to Madame Khokhlakova to discover what has really happened. She gives an account, reminiscent of Fyodor's disquisition about the hooks in hell, that offers a parodic rehashing of the novel's major themes: "If he hasn't murdered me, but only his own father, it's only because the finger of God preserved me [and because] I put the holy icon . . . on his neck. . . . I don't believe in miracles . . . but this unmistakable miracle . . . shakes me. . . . Have you heard about Father Zosima?" (*BK*, 424).

As the mystery plot of the novel intensifies, Dostoevsky increasingly asks the reader to take on the task of weighing the significance of the many facts that come to light and, perhaps, into dispute. Such facts as whether or not the garden gate was open, why Mitya paused in his flight to wipe Grigory's head with his handkerchief, where Mitya got his money, how much money he actually had—all these crucial pieces of evidence must form a whole in order to solve the riddle. And an inquisitive, involved, careful reader will probably at this point turn back to such key chapters as "In the dark" and "A sudden resolution."

But by the time readers reach the chapters (3, 4, and 5) devoted to the three torments of Mitya's soul, they come face to face with a metaphysical riddle superimposed on a mystery plot. What are Mitya's three torments? These three chapters form, on a first reading, or even a second, a continuous unit. Neither Dostoevsky nor the narrator-chronicler, nor even Mitya himself, gives us a clue about what each of these torments is. As we did in reading Book VIII, it becomes useful to turn back to Book III, to those chapters where Mitya made his three-part confession to Alyosha. These chapters hold a clue to Mitya's three torments in Book IX.

Both these tripartite sections begin in the third chapters of their respective books. Moreover, chapter 2 of Book III gave us the story of "Stinking Lizaveta" and chapter 2 of Book IX recapitulates the themes of that story indirectly: Mitya climbs the garden fence in the identical place where Lizaveta had so many years before when she was giving birth to Smerdyakov. And again Marfa Ignatyeva hears groans. " 'Good Lord! Just as it was with Lizaveta Smerdyashchaya,' she thought" (*BK*, 428).

What correspondences and contrasts can we find between Mitya's three-part confession and his three-part torment? (According to Russian Orthodoxy, a soul suffers 40 days of torment after death before it can reach its destination and a resolution.) First and foremost, in Book III Mitya had unburdened his heart to Alyosha, an interlocutor who believes in and loves him. In Book IX Mitya suffers the torment, overarching all three parts, of confessing to those who do not believe him, who do not love him. Alyosha is a messenger, an agent, of God; the Book IX interlocutors represent temporal justice with all its limitations.

Mitya's first torment is the horror and despair he feels in believing that he has murdered Grigory. Upon learning that Grigory is alive, Mitya prays, "Lord, I thank thee for the miracle Thou hast wrought for me, a sinner and an evil doer." We learn that Mitya understands that Grigory has been a true, if not a biological father to him. "He used to wash me in the tub . . . he was like a father to me!" (*BK*, 433). To have killed him, Mitya knows, would have been an act of virtual parricide. In Mitya's earlier confession in verse he had quoted Schiller, and the chapter had closed with Mitya's statement about God and the devil fighting within the heart of man. He had then turned abruptly "to facts" (*BK*, 97). Here in Book IX Mitya literally lays open to view the battle that has been going on in his own heart. He tells his interlocutors that he knows there are "terrible facts" against him (*BK*, 435). The chapter closes with a similar turning away from lofty statements to the facts of the matter. "To business, gentlemen, to business, and don't rummage in my soul . . . only ask me about facts" (*BK*, 438).

Mitya's second torment revolves around, as he sees it, his desperate quest to redeem his lost honor by obtaining 3,000 rubles. He tells his questioners that he needed "to pay a debt of honor, but to whom I won't say." The second part of his confession to Alyosha had also focused on the question of honor, and by the end of it, of course, he had played the role of the man of honor by giving Katerina Ivanovna the money, and she had departed in his debt (chapter 4, Book III). In chapter 4 of Book IX Mitya, as he had earlier, recounts numerous scenarios. The difficulty is that now, instead of being merely ideas, he has actually in desperation just enacted all the scenarios he must now describe. In another reversal, all have involved an attempt to pay *his* debt to Katerina Ivanovna. Thus, although both chapters revolve around the mutually interacting themes of honor and the paying of debts, the events in Book IX are a reversal of those in Book III.

In Book IX Mitya twice quotes a line from Dostoevsky's favorite poem by Fyodor Tiutchev, "Silentium." The most famous line of this poem, which Mitya does not in fact quote but which Dostoevsky's contemporary readers would have known by heart, is "The thought once uttered is lie." And indeed, throughout all of Book IX words play terrible tricks on Mitya. His propensity to spout possible scenarios combines with his anger and impatience to create an entangling web. He himself observes, "Oh, you know how one says the wrong thing without meaning it" (*BK*, 461). Mitya's uttered words are a dense mixture of lies and truth, and although the informed reader may be able to sort them out, the prosecutors, and later the jury, will not.

In Book III the third part of Mitya's confession (chapter 5) had abruptly, with a corresponding shift in genre, opened into the present. "You understand the first half. That half is a drama. . . . The second half is a tragedy, and it is being acted here" (*BK*, 104). The same sudden opening into the novelistic present occurs in chapter 5 of Book IX, "The third torment." Mitya's account reaches the moment of the murder. First, with wrath, Mitya says, "I murdered him"; then he gives his real account. "Whether it was someone's tears, or my mother prayed to God, or a good angel kissed me at that instant, I don't know. But the devil was conquered" (*BK,* 446). Zosima's mysterious visitor, despite his overriding resemblance to Ivan, bears a powerful resemblance to Mitya here. He confesses that he had come perilously close to killing Zosima, but that murder, as with Mitya, does not occur. "The Lord vanquished the devil in my heart," says the mysterious visitor (*BK,* 291). Even at this crucial moment in Mitya's life, moreover, he is ironically aware, just as he was in Book III, of both his own narrative abilities and the creative potential of the moment he is describing. "A poem! In verse!" (*BK,* 446).

By this time in our reading of the novel nearly every word of Mitya's statement exists in an envelope of meaning: his words possess an aura of special significance based on all that has gone before. Thus his statement constitutes one of those intense spiritual nodules in the text which can only be perceived in the context of the symbols and mythologies that have gradually developed up to this point. "Someone's tears" suggests the interconnectedness of events, Zosima's great ocean, the tears of the grieving peasant mother, and so on. "My mother prayed to God," "a good angel kissed me," "the devil was conquered"—each of these phrases resonates through the entire novel. To unravel the many reverberations present in this rich tangle of phrases would be to restate the entire novel. Suffice it to say, each of Mitya's words possesses tremendous significance for the novel as a whole.

Specifically, his words about the devil recall the famous closing passage of chapter 4, Book III. "The awful thing is that beauty is mysterious as well as terrible. God and the devil are fighting there and the battlefield is the heart of man. But a man always talks of his own ache" (*BK,* 97). Perhaps in Mitya's heart, at least, that crucial battle has been waged. Mitya's confession to Alyosha had closed with his repeated assertions that he believes in miracles. Yet amid these protestations of faith had lurked the dark hint that he might yet murder his father. Mitya's third torment embodies this same unresolved tension: he will not reveal where he got the money or how much of it he has. In both chapters Mitya ignores the mass of negative and positive human expectations swirling around him and simply gives himself up, in a recklessly passive way, to the ripples of divine providence eddying around him.

When Mitya finally reveals his great secret—that he had not spent all of Katerina Ivanovna's 3,000 rubles on the first debauch but had saved 1,500 rubles, which he had just now been spending at Mokroe—he has, by his own code of honor, made the most difficult confession of all. As true confessions typically manifest themselves in Dostoevsky's fiction, the significance of his words passes virtually unnoticed. Later Mitya asks, "Why, why did I degrade myself by confessing my secret to you?" (*BK*, 470). (And Mitya's words are, of course, being transcribed as evidence against him, even as he speaks.)

Ippolit Kirillovich, the prosecutor at Mitya's trial, even minimizes their importance, for he sees no disgrace, simply recklessness, in Mitya's act. Yet for Mitya the 1,500 rubles represent the very crux of the matter. "It's not the fifteen hundred that's the disgrace, but that I put it apart from the rest of the three thousand. . . . I was calculating" (*BK*, 464). We learn that Mitya is more tortured by the thought that he has been a thief than by the thought that he might have, in a fit of fury, murdered Grigory. Mitya's judgment of himself has a Dantesque cast to it, for in Dante's hell those who are guilty of willful and premeditated fraud are even more guilty than those who have murdered out of passion.

The circumstantial evidence against Mitya mounts relentlessly. The crucial piece of evidence that could help him—the amulet into which he had put the money—has vanished in the marketplace, thrown carelessly there by Mitya as he ran from Grushenka's frightened servant Fenya to Perkhotin's. The innkeeper asserts that Mitya definitely must have spent at least 3,000 rubles on his first spree alone. The moving account by Andrey, the peasant driver, of his conversation with Mitya on the road likewise becomes fodder for Ippolit Kirillovich's psychological theories. The young Kalganov unwillingly supports the innkeeper's view, as do, of course, the two Poles. Poor old Maximov declares that Mitya must have been holding 20,000 rubles in his hand, and even Grushenka, despite her firm belief that Mitya is innocent of murder, also believes, like the innkeeper, that Mitya had spent a full 3,000 rubles on his first spree alone.

When the exhausted Mitya falls asleep, he has a visionary dream that constitutes a kind of conversion experience and, through its emphasis on the suffering of a child, also links him to Ivan, Alyosha, and Zosima. All four characters stand transfixed before the spectacle of a suffering child, for all four of them experience intense pain at the thought of such suffering. Moreover, for all four the possibility for religious faith is inextricably and mysteriously intertwined with the reality of such suffering.

In Mitya's dream elements already familiar to us abound. Water in the form not of tears but of snow touches the earth. A mother whose breasts have no milk holds her shivering, crying baby. Mitya repeatedly asks his peasant driver and guide why the babe is weeping. He knows his questions are unreasonable and unanswerable, yet he is overcome by a passion of pity and a desire to "do something for them all, so that the babe should weep no more" (*BK,* 479). He then imagines he hears Grushenka's voice beside him, promising to stay with him always. The image of the suffering child, which has provoked the agony of Ivan's rebellion, awakens in Mitya the desire—even if it is unreasoning, senseless, ridiculous—to acknowledge his responsibility to his fellow man. What engenders this dream? Is it the knowledge that Grigory is alive? Is it Grushenka's faith in him? Or is it the anonymous kindness of the person who has placed a pillow beneath his head and, in doing so, may have handed him that onion by which he could pull himself from the abyss?

Again, as with Alyosha's vision of Cana of Galilee and his subsequent tears in the garden, this key moment for Mitya seems to have precursors that are as important as the dream itself. The night before, he had, in reality, been on the road to Mokroe with a peasant driver, Andrey. Mitya had suddenly asked him, "Tell me, will Dmitri Fyodorovich go to hell or not?" (*BK,* 389). Andrey had replied with yet another story about a visit to hell. This time it is the Son of God who visits hell after his crucifixion and sets free the sinners suffering there. And again, as in Zosima's reading of the Book of Job, as in Ivan's recitation about the Grand Inquisitor, and as in Grushenka's fable of the onion, we see God and the devil locked in a kind of contest with each other.

Mitya is pleased by this peasant legend of the harrowing of hell. Andrey then assures Mitya that he will not go to hell, for he is like a little child. Suddenly Mitya asks Andrey to forgive him, "for everyone, for everyone, you here alone, on the road, will you forgive me for everyone?" (*BK,* 389). As we saw with Alyosha, Grushenka's fable of the onion, and its subsequent relationship to his vision of Cana of Galilee, we see in this episode with the peasant on the road a miniature, yet powerful preenactment, or rehearsal, of the main event—the dream of the babe. In retrospect, this earlier moment, as with Alyosha, has as much significance as the moment it prefigures and engenders.

This incident with Andrey on the road also recalls a key moment in Zosima's *Life* in a powerful and haunting way. We have already remarked on the correspondence between the young Zosima and Mitya. Both men had struck their servants (Afanasy and Grigory), and this violent act became part of a chain of events precipitating a spiritual conversion: the swashbuckling romantic hero suddenly decides, authentically, to live for others. This incident with Andrey on the road also resembles that key moment of Zosima's preconversion conversion, after he has struck Afanasy. Like Zosima, Mitya asks forgiveness of a peasant who becomes baffled and alarmed by the sudden change in him. "Oh Sir! I feel afraid of driving you, your talk is so strange" (*BK*, 389).

7

Varieties of Guilty Experience
PART IV: BOOKS X, XI, XII, AND THE EPILOGUE

Although Mitya's epiphanic vision of the babe occurs in August, it had been set in a dream landscape "early in November" (*v nachale noyabr'*) (*BK*, 478). The next book of the novel, Book X, "The Boys," opens with the words, "It was the beginning of November" (*Noyabr' v nachale*) (*BK*, 486). The month of November plays a key role in many of Dostoevsky's fictional works, from *The Double* to *The Brothers Karamazov*, and has a mysterious link with the phenomenon of spiritual crisis—as indeed it does in this novel for Mitya, for Ivan in Book XI, and for Kolya Krasotkin here in Book X. In this book God and the devil wage a battle (in Dostoevsky's terms and in Mitya's as well) in Kolya's heart, and by the end of the book he will have passed through his own spiritual gauntlet. Curiously, Mitya actually has his dream in August— the time of Alyosha's epiphany—but because it is set in November it is linked with Ivan's and Kolya's crises, which both occur in November.

BOOK X

Book X is my own favorite in the novel. Here we see the weightiest, most theologically and philosophically difficult problems of the novel transpose themselves into a new mode of expression. Kolya Krasotkin, Ilyusha Snegiryov, and the other boys double, reenact, enlarge upon, and rework many of the novel's major themes while also illustrating, in a convincing yet simple fashion, what Zosima had meant when he uttered the seeming platitude, "All is like an ocean, all is flowing and blending; a touch in one place sets up movement at the other end of the earth" (*BK*, 299). Here our earth is a small village; nevertheless, the chains of movement are unexpected.

At the beginning of Part IV, the last part of the novel, the narrator-chronicler steps back from his dramatic plot, regroups his forces, and presents us with a whole sheaf of new introductory material. Is this new direction a digression or a working out of the central themes of the novel? Certainly Dostoevsky had been chastised in the past by his critics for putting too many episodes and plots into his novels. And he had replied with uncharacteristic defensiveness and apologies. Nearly 10 years earlier he had admitted to his friend, the critic and journalist Nikolai Strakhov, "I am utterly incapable (something I never learned) of controlling my material. Many separate novels and novellas get squeezed into a single one so that there is no proportion and no harmony" (*Letters*, 359).[1]

But clearly Dostoevsky did not really mean to change his ways. Indeed, this connectedness through diffusion lies at the heart of both his artistic and his theological vision. As we have seen, the bedrock of Dostoevsky's creativity is his perception of the multiplicity embedded in a unity in which, to use Bakhtin's phraseology, dialogism or polyphony exists at the most primary level. The atoms of Dostoevsky's art contain, like real atoms, both a positive and a negative charge (God and the devil, good and evil, a beautiful and a disfigured image) to complete their quivering, precarious "neutrality."[2]

Just as the story of Zosima's past doubles aspects of the lives of Alyosha, Ivan, and Mitya, so does the story of the boys reflect that of the Karamazov brothers, even as it is, in terms of the mechanisms of the plot, a direct result or ramification of the brothers' actions. As the next generation the boys point the way to the future in the same way that Zosima forms a link to the past (even though he was both prophet and prophecy of the future). But all three groups are responsible for each other and are linked—both literally, through the plot, and figuratively, through a shared metaphoric perception of life and death.

Kolya combines occasional echoes of Mitya with a powerful resemblance to Ivan. At the same time, however, he is a true child. Through this charming boy, who exists as a full-fledged creation in his own right, Dostoevsky thus offers a new refraction of aspects of Mitya, Ivan, and the Grand Inquisitor.

As readers, we have by now become sensitive to the many parodies that exist in this novel. The ones we have seen so far have often been wickedly or darkly humorous. An unsavory character like Fyodor, Smerdyakov, or Rakitin spews out a "problem" or a "paradox" that then receives a serious, genuinely problematic or paradoxical treatment. But now, having passed through the novel's dense metaphysical and philosophical core, the reader suddenly comes face to face with a new kind of parody, a delightful, though serious one. In fact, in our enjoyment of Kolya's antics it is easy to miss the dark seriousness lurking behind them and the dreadful significance his deeds have for the insulted and injured Ilyusha.

Like Ivan, Kolya actively seeks knowledge in order to impress his peers. Like Ivan, Kolya has affection for children; we see him as a responsible babysitter, a "protector" of children. Kolya resembles the Grand Inquisitor in many of the ways that Ivan himself does. Kolya possesses secret knowledge—whether about the identities of the founders of Troy or the identity of a mangy, shaggy dog—that secures his power over his "flock" even as it isolates him and causes him suffering.

The events of Book X occur over the space of a single morning, a morning that proves to be a turning point in the lives of both Kolya and Ilyusha. Along the way, Kolya offers up a multifaceted confession to Alyosha, much as Mitya and Ivan had done before him (and as the mysterious visitor had with Zosima). Moreover, Alyosha, whom the reader has not seen for two books, two months, and many pages, has changed, the narrator-chronicler is quick to assure us (*BK*, 503). The epiphanic rapture he experienced in his vision of Cana of Galilee and its aftermath in the garden seem to have remained with him. He is no longer dressed as a novice, and his good-humored face also bespeaks an increased gentleness and serenity (*BK*, 503).

As they do with both Mitya and Ivan, women find Kolya charming. He also shares the brothers' predilection for literary language and for making generalizations about children, Russians, religion, and the workings of the human heart. He, like them, finds himself irresistibly drawn to and fond of Alyosha. Both Mitya and Ivan have struggled and continue to struggle mightily with the warring factions in their hearts. A war rages within Kolya, too.

Many critics have taken note of Kolya's quite striking affinities with Ivan and the Grand Inquisitor. Before passing on to these, I would like to glance at some refractions of Mitya in Kolya. Mitya sets in motion one of the darkest, most tragic plots of the novel by pulling Captain Snegiryov's beard and humiliating him in front of Ilyusha and the boys. This public act of insult precipitates the stone throwing and Ilyusha's injury. Stones, like seeds, like psychology, like miracles, like virtually every indirect repository of meaning in the novel, become an image, as we have seen, that possesses both a negative and a positive charge. These stones wound; others will heal. Jesus refused to change the stones into bread because he would not purchase man's belief that way. But within this novel stones produce a nourishment of their own.

Kolya, like Mitya, purposefully commits an act of insult involving a beard. "The peasant's beard's frozen,' Kolya cried in a loud provocative voice as he passed him" (*BK*, 498). He also shares Mitya's propensity for being a deliberate narrator, capable of exaggerating his misfortune in order to please his audience. "What would a schoolboy be, if he were not whipped? And if I were to tell him we are not, he'd be disappointed. . . . One has to know how to talk to the peasants" (*BK*, 499).

Moreover, like Mitya, Kolya is, in his childish way, given to public brawling and has provoked more anger against himself than he realizes. "He had been in so many rows on the street that he could hardly remember them all" (*BK*, 499). Mitya, on the road to Mokroe, had, like Zosima before him, stunned and embarrassed a peasant by asking for his forgiveness. Kolya's third encounter in the marketplace, on his way to Ilyusha, resonates with this incident. Mitya's asking of forgiveness had occurred spontaneously as he was on his way to Mokroe to stir up trouble; Kolya tells young Smurov that he likes "to stir up fools in every class of society." He then sees a drunken peasant and starts to mock him. The peasant replies, "Well, God forgive you." And Kolya finds himself asking, "Do you forgive me, too?" "I quite forgive you. Go along" (*BK*, 501). Dostoevsky deftly sounds the same theme in two very different keys. The metaphysical, lofty moment in the dark on the road to Mokroe gives way to the world of mischievous boys, impatient adults, and the bustle of the marketplace. But the fundamental notes and rhythms are the same.

Like Mitya, Kolya is a skillful and incisive narrator. Mitya, in his confession to Alyosha, had told us his story and analyzed his own psychological motivations as well as the narrator-chronicler or even Dostoevsky himself could have done. Kolya offers Alyosha a similarly powerful narration; at last we hear the full account of his relationship with Ilyusha.

Moreover, Kolya, like Mitya, precipitates unhappiness and tragedy by a vitally significant act of withholding. Mitya had withheld the remaining portion of the money he owed Katerina Ivanovna and had kept it secretly in a bag around his neck. Kolya withholds the dog Zhuchka from Ilyusha. Each act of holding back emanates from a destructive attraction to self-dramatization. Each character awaits the perfect moment to reveal his secret; each waits too long. However perceptive Mitya and Kolya are as narrators of their respective stories, they each, through the vanity of showmanship, commit a serious error in timing.

But this vanity, Alyosha realizes, is no small matter. Mitya fears losing his honor; Kolya fears being ridiculous. Both are vain. The devil and God battle in each of their hearts, and Alyosha intones the presence of the devil in a literal way that serves also to forecast his appearance to Ivan in Book XI. "The devil has taken the form of that vanity and entered into the whole generation; it's simply the devil, added Alyosha, without a trace of the smile that Kolya, staring at him, expected to see. 'You are like everyone else' " (*BK*, 526). Both Mitya and Kolya are deeply guilty before the Snegiryov family; each has caused Ilyusha to suffer. For each, genuine tears and repentance finally come. Mitya dreams of the babe, for whom he will undertake imprisonment; Kolya at last weeps, without shame, for the dying Ilyusha. Dostoevsky has instilled and recast much of his huge novel into his seemingly direct account of the unfolding of events on a single November morning, the day before Mitya's trial is to begin.

After endowing Kolya with all these resemblances to Mitya, it is a stunning achievement on the part of Dostoevsky, a true sleight of hand, that Kolya should have even more links to Ivan than he does to Mitya. Like Ivan, Kolya frequently displays a tendency toward inflated language; he loves to make generalizations, to quote writers like Belinsky and Voltaire, even if, unlike Ivan, he has not read them. Kolya also seeks to reject God's world, even as he proclaims his love for mankind in general. Despite his proclamations of love for man, he has offended against particular men, specifically against Ilyusha.

Both Ivan and Kolya had longed "to make Alyosha's acquaintance." Each doubter is irresistibly drawn to the angelic believer and wants to show himself at his best. Each proclaims to Aloysha with pride, and as a kind of bedrock to his being, his love of children. "I am always fond of children," says Kolya (*BK*, 503). Yet of more immediate importance to the world of this novel, and thus more harrowing than Ivan's dreadful litany of the tortures inflicted on children, is the fact that the appealing Kolya is in fact himself a torturer of children, for he inflicts unjustified suffering on Ilyusha.

Ivan had smilingly observed to Alyosha that every Russian school-boy loves to discuss the eternal questions. Kolya is himself that school-boy, yet he also loves to talk—in a scene that has both a delicious and a poignant irony for the reader—about Russian schoolboys. He converses with Alyosha, and gradually, as it had been with Ivan, Kolya realizes that "our talk has been like a declaration of love" (*BK*, 527). Their encounter ends not with a kiss but with an affectionate pressing of hands.

Like Ivan, Kolya has a theory he wishes to work out and to verify. But whereas Ivan's theories are about the right to commit and punish crime, Kolya's theory is about Alyosha. His language is familiar: "Karamazov's a riddle to me. . . . I have a theory about him which I must work out and verify" (*BK*, 497). Both Ivan and Kolya like to explain things in the current fashionable language of discourse, which favors phrases like "the laws of nature." We have already seen that Kolya's encounters with the peasants in the marketplace recapitulate Mitya's experience, but typical of Dostoevsky's economy as a writer, they foreshadow Ivan's experience as well. In Book XI Ivan too will encounter a peasant who combines elements of the three peasants with whom Kolya speaks: Ivan's peasant will be freezing (like the peasant with the frozen beard), angry, and drunk.

Ivan, as we have seen, narrated his poem to Alyosha, who had given back to him the glowing kiss that his fictional Jesus had planted upon his Grand Inquisitor's lips. The story Kolya tells to Alyosha is no exalted poem; it is more in the spirit of Mitya's narrative, though Kolya, like Ivan, tests out his ideas in the course of it. And Kolya and Alyosha do have a discussion about art—not about poetry, as Ivan and Alyosha did, but about theatrical performances. Alyosha praises Kolya for not hesitating to "play horsey" with the younger children. Alyosha's views on art here echo those of Plato, Rousseau, and even Dostoevsky's old adversary, Nikolai Chernyshevsky. "Sometimes [children's] games are much better than performances in the theatre . . . in these games the young people are the actors themselves" (*BK*, 508). Moreover, in the narrative about Ilyusha that Kolya gives, he himself is the leading actor. Ivan's poem rendered a hypothetical story; Kolya becomes a literal Grand Inquisitor and himself enacts, within his own childish world, a scenario not unlike that of Ivan's literary creation.

As Book XI unfolds, we will be asked to consider the difficult question of the extent to which Ivan is guilty as the inciter of evil action. Smerdyakov has been both a petty devil to him, in the role of instigator of evil, and his lackey, his willing evil agent. Here we learn that Smerdyakov has acted in the former capacity for Ilyusha as well. Yet it is Kolya who incites an act of murder, though only of a goose. He tempts a peasant (an errand boy of twenty) to prove a silly theory ("If that cart were to move on a little, would it break the goose's neck or not?"); he instigates an evil action, thus entering into the dark realms inhabited by Smerdyakov and Ivan. "I winked at the lad, he tugged at the bridle, and crack! The goose's neck was broken in half." As Ivan will do in Book XII, Kolya then tells how he and the peasant appeared before a judge. He reiterates the peasant's angry words of blame: "And the fellow kept blubbering like a woman. 'It wasn't me,' he said, 'it was he who egged me on,' and he pointed to me. I answered with the utmost composure that I hadn't egged him on, that I simply stated the general proposition, had spoken hypothetically" (*BK*, 518). What is this but a parodic foreshadowing of Smerdyakov's dreadful words to Ivan: "You murdered him; you are the real murderer, I was only your instrument, your faithful servant Licharda, and it was following your words I did it" (*BK*, 590).

These parallels between Ivan and Smerdyakov and between Kolya and the errand boy at Plotnikov's are dramatic, although there is a crucial difference between them: when Ivan at last appears before a judge, his composure is completely shattered. In both cases, however, the judge or court utterly fails to see the significance of the role of instigator. Kolya's judge merely smiles at the prank; he promises to complain to Kolya's teacher, but he never does so. Likewise, the court totally misreads Ivan's confession. In both cases the temporal arbitrators of justice fail. As a curious footnote to these weightier matters about the dispensation of justice in the courts, we also learn that Ivan and Kolya are the two characters in *The Brothers Karamazov* for whom the railroads—always a source of negative imagery in Dostoevsky's work—play a role. Kolya had gained power and authority over the boys partly through his mad courage in lying on the railroad tracks as a train passed over him. And Ivan had taken the train to Moscow just before his father's murder. "I am a scoundrel," he had whispered to himself. Kolya comes to the same realization. "I am a scoundrel in lots of ways, Karamazov" (*BK*, 526).

Three of Kolya's most significant actions—lying under the train, inciting the murder of the goose, and attempting to create a miracle by bringing back to life at the right moment the "dead" dog Zhuchka—parody and reflect Ivan's actions and ideas. This doubling is particularly subtle and convincing because Ivan and Kolya, despite their uncanny resemblance to each other, have never met.

The use to which Kolya would put his "secret knowledge" also connects him with Ivan's Grand Inquisitor. Indeed, his resemblances to the Inquisitor are at least as numerous as his resemblances to Ivan. Kolya, we see, is a liar—a charming liar, but a liar nevertheless. His considerable rhetorical power combines with his lies in a manner reminiscent of the Grand Inquisitor. At the beginning of the novel we were reminded by Fyodor that the devil is the father of lies; Kolya within the mundane confines of his village sphere and life as a child, has succumbed to the devil's three temptations just as has the lofty, fictional Grand Inquisitor of Seville. Like him, Kolya lies to the children to maintain his authority over them and to create his own aura of miracle and mystery.

Kolya wields his authority over the children through the wonder of his toy cannon, through his secret knowledge of the founders of Troy, and through his charisma. Throughout Book X Kolya is attempting to orchestrate—at the expedient time, as he mistakenly conceives it—his own miracle. When Jesus appeared on the scene in Ivan's poem, he had raised up a dead child. Kolya, too, tries to create a raising of the dead. Early on he tells Smurov, "Zhuchka doesn't exist. Zhuchka is lost in the mists of obscurity." Smurov wishes they could pretend that Kolya's new dog Perezvon is Zhuchka (which, of course, he is), and Kolya, even as he is lying about Perezvon's identity, confidently and condescendingly exhorts, "Boy, shun a lie, that's one thing; even with a good object, that's another" (*BK, 496*).

Throughout, Kolya proudly displays Perezvon's tricks. The one of which he is proudest is Perezvon's talent for playing dead. "Be dead, be dead" runs as a kind of refrain through these pages, and Kolya is the "only one" (*BK, 514*) who can raise him. Kolya, moreover, pretends that the real Zhuchka is dead and brings him to life by an act of will in an effort to impress, forgive, and heal Ilyusha. His "miracle" of raising the dead bears no fruit: Ilyusha, the object of his torture and his love, dies.

The Grand Inquisitor reverberates in other ways through Book X. Jesus refuses to turn the stones into bread. We have already seen how the boys throw stones at each other; yet more destructive even than the stone throwing is the bread throwing. Smerdyakov, in his guise as tempting devil, teaches Ilyusha to put a pin in bread and to toss it to dogs. It is Ilyusha's fear that he has murdered Zhuchka that first propels him to despair. Smerdyakov thus literalizes the devil's temptation, for, as Jesus realizes, stones turned into bread to buy men's faith would offer men no real nourishment—such bread would be equivalent to bread with a pin in it.

Moreover, when Ilyusha confesses his sin to the child inquisitor Kolya, his intermediary before God, Kolya does precisely what Ivan's article had advocated and what Zosima, with his loving heart, had argued so passionately against: he "excommunicates" Ilyusha, he casts him out from the brotherhood of boys. As Zosima had predicted, being cut off has terrible results: Ilyusha's despair bears fruit. He stabs Kolya with the penknife; he bites Alyosha; he cries out in anger, "I will throw bread with pins to all the dogs—all—all of them" (*BK*, 505).

Just as Ivan's narrative, his poem of rebellion and rejection, had seemed to be, as Alyosha observed, indirectly in praise of Jesus rather than in blame of him, so too does Kolya's narrative to Alyosha work at cross-purposes to itself. He sets out to justify his course of action, but the sheer power of Ilyusha's grief, despair, and victimization, as Kolya describes it, subverts his own account. Ilyusha's tears pierce our hearts, and when we learn from Alyosha that Ilyusha has three times repeated, tearfully, "It's because I killed Zhuchka, dad, that I am ill now. God is punishing me for it" (*BK*, 506), we realize with immediacy, rather than in theory, that it is folly to claim, as many in the monastery had upon Zosima's death, that one can see the finger of God in a particular event.

Moreover, throughout much of Kolya's narrative Alyosha remains silent. "Alyosha had looked serious and had not said a word all the time. . . . Alyosha was still silent" (*BK*, 519). Alyosha's silence echoes that of Jesus, as well as his own silence during most of Ivan's narrative. When Alyosha finally does speak to Kolya, he says, with a faint smile, "I don't agree." Ivan and Kolya both, as we have already seen, end their narratives with assertions of their love for Alyosha (*BK*, 244, 528).

In the last chapter of Book X, Dostoevsky, as he had done in chapter 3 of Book II and as he will do again at the end of the novel, pulls out all the stops and creates a narrative tour de force. The themes of the death of a child, seeds, tears, memory, and the overarching paradox of the Book of Job all coalesce. Kolya's tears at last come with full force; tears engulf Ilyusha, his father, and many readers as well. Ilyusha tries to comfort his father, "Dad, don't cry, and when I die get a good boy, another one. . . . But don't forget me, dad, . . . come to my grave in the evening . . . and dad, bury me by our big stone" (*BK*, 530). Each of his words has a special meaning endowed to it by the act of reading the novel. The incantatory language recalls the peasant woman who had lost her baby, yet here the dying child himself comforts the grieving parent; Ilyusha's weeping and his words "don't cry" embody the paradox of Zosima's advice to her—first telling her not to weep, then telling her to do so. Memory, stones, the end of the day, and the setting sun are the living molecules of grace, as Dostoevsky understood it, and are all present.

As Kolya tearfully curses himself, Dostoevsky offers up his own recasting of the story of Job and his torments. Captain Snegiryov echoes the passion of Ivan in his refusal to accept any future solution to the problem of the suffering of children. But where Ivan's agony was spiritual, the captain's involves every aspect of his being, for he is actually losing his child; he is enduring the torments of Job. "I don't want a good boy! I don't want another boy." He repeats the words of Psalm 137:5–6, "If I forget thee, Jerusalem, may my tongue. . . ." With Captain Snegiryov and Ilyusha, Dostoevsky brings the metaphysical problems that have functioned at an analytical or anecdotal level— whether from philosophy or the Bible—into the very heart of his novel and its plot.

Our likable Kolya unwittingly finds himself, however much he resembles Mitya, Ivan, and the Grand Inquisitor, allied with the awful torturers of children whom Ivan had described. Is forgiveness possible? Dare one forgive? Dostoevsky will reserve the answer to this question until the epilogue. Meanwhile, Kolya leaves Book X seeking a knowledge different from the kind that had engaged him at its beginning. As Captain Snegiryov finds words for his agony through remembering— plagiarizing—the words of the Bible, Kolya asks, "What did he mean by that?" (*BK*, 531).

BOOK XI

It may seem strange that Book V, "Pro and Contra," was not entitled "Ivan," for it is certainly his book. Yet Dostoevsky waits until Book XI to use Ivan's name as a title, for it is only here, as the novel draws to its close, that Ivan goes through a series of crises that result in a transformation comparable to what has already occurred for Alyosha, Mitya, and even Kolya. Book XI brings to the fore many varieties and theories of guilt; each chapter offers up, as it were, a separate meditation on the nature of guilt.

Books X and XI each take place on the day before Mitya's trial is to begin. We already know that whether or not Mitya is guilty of murder, he is certainly guilty of spending a large part of the 3,000 rubles Katerina Ivanovna had entrusted to him. Now, in a nice ironic touch, we learn that Katerina Ivanovna, Ivan, and Alyosha have paid the same sum for a famous Moscow doctor to come to help Mitya. Katerina Ivanovna hopes to prove that Mitya was out of his mind when he committed the murder. Grushenka, on the contrary, steadfastly maintains Mitya's innocence, even as she laments the monumental accumulation of circumstantial evidence pointing to Mitya's guilt.

This mass of incriminating evidence, we learn, has not particularly upset Mitya, for although two months have already passed since his dream of the babe, he has continued in the same softened spiritual state. His concern is with his metaphysical guilt as a man before other men. Grushenka worries that he might be going mad, and she repeats his words to Alyosha: "He suddenly began talking to me about a 'babe'—that is, about some child. 'Why is the babe poor?' he said. 'It's for that babe I am going to Siberia now. I am not a murderer, but I must go to Siberia' " (*BK*, 560). And for the reader perhaps this babe has begun to merge with the dying Ilyusha, before whose father Mitya stands guilty of violence. Yet Mitya remains unconscious of the child who actually lies dying and whose fate is so connected to his own. His focus continues to be on the collective babe of his dream.

Grushenka, unable to keep a secret, reveals that Ivan has already twice visited Mitya in secret and that the two brothers do not want Alyosha to know of these visits. The notion of secret visitors who have secrets to tell recalls Zosima's mysterious visitor, who, as we have already seen, resembled Ivan. Now Ivan himself plays the role of the secret visitor. Secrets have thus far exerted a peculiar force of their own; from the secret knocks on Fyodor's door to the secrets of the soul, they have formed a vital, if obscure link in the chains of action and motivation. But Book XI literally teems and crawls with secrets and their revelations. Ya. E. Golosovker has aptly observed, "It is clear that the word 'secret' is connected with murder, baseness, theft, treachery, false testimony, intrigue, jealousy, and a confusion of thoughts and feelings. Basically, however, the 'secret' turns about the murder of old Karamazov, around that 'devil's deed.' "[3]

When the devil at last makes his appearance in chapter 9, he too arrives as a mysterious visitor, and Ivan becomes, for a change, the one who is visited, much as he had been in the tavern two months earlier by the angelic Alyosha. Moreover, the devil is a mysterious visitor with a secret.

Dostoevsky well knew that Book XI, and particularly its ninth chapter, would prove controversial. He assured his editor that he had consulted with doctors and that they confirmed his artistic intuition:

> Not only nightmares but also hallucinations are possible before bouts of "white fever." . . . It is a question here not only of a physical (pathological) phenomenon, in which a person begins to lose, at times, the ability to distinguish between the real and the imaginary (something that happens to everyone at least once in his life), but also of a psychological trait that is in keeping with the character of my hero. . . . *Suffering as he is from his inability to believe, he at the same time wishes (unconsciously) that the apparition should not be just a figment of his imagination, but something that was actually there* [Dostoevsky's italics]." (*Letters,* 508)

So much for Dostoevsky's "public" statements about Book XI. He claimed the medical accuracy of his account of Ivan's illness; he set the stage carefully for a reading of the crucial chapter as a hallucination— a fantastic episode succeeded, for the reader, by a relieved reentry into the world of everyday reality.

But like the other images and motifs in the novel, this key chapter cuts both ways. Perhaps it is no hallucination. Perhaps the devil is the ultimate mysterious visitor. Perhaps Dostoevsky wishes his readers and Ivan to have a suspicion that the devil himself might actually have come calling. Dostoevsky frequently boasted about his writing style of "fantastic realism." This chapter offers us a splendid example of what Dostoevsky means by the term, as do such works as *The Double*, "The Landlady" (1847), "Bobok" (1873), "The Peasant Marei" (1876), "The Dream of a Ridiculous Man," and parts of all his other novels, particularly *The Idiot*. Key to all these works is the reader's hesitation about how to categorize certain events in them—do they fit within the confines of everyday reality as we usually conceive it, or are they moments of fantasy, of the marvelous? Dostoevsky, like other practitioners of the fantastic, counts precisely upon this hesitation; to produce it successfully in a reader is to achieve a state of "fantastic realism"—to recast, albeit only momentarily, one's sense of the nature of reality.

Varieties of Guilty Experience

In the second chapter of Book XI Madame Khokhlakova comically expounds her own latest theory of guilt, or its lack—"aberration." Her ideas, distilled from those of the visiting Moscow doctor and her own shaky understanding of the recent reforms in court law (to which Dostoevsky was opposed and which he satirizes here), come close to being a ridiculous parody of Ivan's own atheistic aphorism—ironically borrowed from the Bible—"everything is permitted." Madame Khokhlakova defines her term for Alyosha in its "legal sense." "An aberration in which everything is pardonable. Whatever you do, you will be acquitted at once." Dostoevsky lets her go on to parody his own cherished idea of all men's shared guilt toward and responsibility for one another. "And besides, who isn't suffering from aberration nowadays?—You, I, all of us are in a state of aberration. . . . Why, my Lise is in a state of aberration" (*BK*, 545, 547). In Ivan's formulation, "everything is permitted"; there is, likewise, no guilt and no responsibility. In Madame Khokhlakova's theory of aberration, we are all, on the contrary, guilty. But no one need feel responsible for this guilt; it simply does not matter.

It turns out that Ivan has secretly been visiting Lise Khokhlakova as well as Mitya. These secret visits have propelled her into a hysterical frenzy. Finally, Madame Khokhlakova reveals to Alyosha that Lise had insulted and then begged forgiveness from her servant. All these events—secret visits, hysterical fits, begging forgiveness from insulted servants—rhyme with others in the novel and are particularly suggestive of Mitya, Katerina Ivanovna, and Zosima. Madame Khokhlakova's comic theory of aberration, a theory which combines the work of the custodians of temporal power—doctors and lawyers—with her own silliness, gives way to a much more problematic parody of the novel's ideas about guilt. The next chapter, "A little demon," functions as a preface for chapter 9.

Lise's mother outlines a theory of aberration that acknowledges guilt but denies that anyone need really take responsibility for it. Lise, on the other hand, puts forth a theory that acknowledges that everyone is responsible for evil, but that also asserts no one need feel guilty about it: "Everyone loves crime, they love it always, not at some 'moments.' . . . you know it's as though people have made an agreement to lie about it. . . . They all declare that they hate evil, but secretly they all love it" (*BK*, 551). Her approach reflects the lacerating seeking out of guilt in order to take a voluptuous pleasure in it. Moreover, like Father Ferapont, Lise dreams of devils, "devils all over the place . . . a crowd of them" (*BK*, 551). To her surprise, and ours,

Alyosha admits that he has had the same dream. Thus Ferapont, Lise, and Alyosha—an unlikely trio—all presage Ivan's hallucination in a way that works against the physical preparation for it in the growing signs of Ivan's illness. The combined effect of these forebodings is to inject a heavy dose of the fantastic into the reality of the novel.

Alyosha, surprisingly, finds much to agree with in Lise's words. " 'There is some truth in what you say about everyone,' he answers her softly" (*BK, 551*). Her theoretical depiction of universal responsibility for evil with no need for anyone to feel guilty about it—indeed, loving it instead—is in fact a way of claiming to value aesthetic form without any moral content. This notion hearkens back to Mitya's earlier lamentation over men confusing the beauty of Sodom with that of the Madonna. This Gothic vision of corrupted beauty finds its dreadful formal apotheosis in the horrible verbal icon of disfigurement that Lise puts forth to Alyosha. This icon possesses a harmonious aesthetic form that is hideously at odds with its dreadful content. It is an aesthetic manifestation of the war taking place in the human spirit. Lise describes her vision of a mutilated child who has been crucified by a "Jew." The child moans for four hours before it dies. Her aesthetic evaluation of the scene is that it is "nice" (*BK, 552*). Sharing the twisted desire for punishment and martyrdom of Stavrogin (*The Possessed*) and Dostoevsky's "ridiculous man" ("The Dream of a Ridiculous Man"), she adds, "I sometimes imagine that it was I who crucified him. He would hang there moaning and I would sit opposite him eating pineapple compote" (*BK, 552*).

This is, perhaps, the moral low point of the novel. Dostoevsky devastatingly illustrates here how evil seeds can take root in anyone's heart, even in the heart of a child like Lise. Sadly, the seal of aesthetic approval—the word *nice*—had been given to Lise by Ivan, whom she describes only as "he" or "a certain person." Her refusal to use his name at this crucial juncture would intimate to Dostoevsky's contemporary readers Ivan's connection to the devil. For the devil in Russian folklore is also traditionally not named but rather simply described as "he."

Both Ivan and his disciple Lise are believers "in the pineapple compote"; hence, each is ill. "Save me!" Lise suddenly cries out to Alyosha (*BK, 553*). Lise's aesthetic temptation toward evil meshes with Kolya's intellectual, ideological temptations toward atheism and feigned miracle for utilitarian purposes. It also meshes with Ilyusha's temptation to evil, that of the injured and insulted child who, in his despair, wants to throw pin-infested bread to all the dogs. Through these three children, each of whom the reader cares for, Dostoevsky offers the reader difficult and painful examples of his belief that children are not exempt from the temptation and allure of evil.

The third chapter of Book IV had ended with Ilyusha concluding his interview with Alyosha by biting Alyosha's finger to the bone and thereby desperately wounding himself. The third chapter of Book XI also concludes with a finger being wounded at the end of an encounter with Alyosha: Lise injures not Alyosha's finger but her own. She deliberately puts her finger in the crack of the door and slams the door on it. Her last words echo those of Ivan and Kolya: she whispers about herself, "Base, base, base" (*podlaya*) (*BK, 554*).

The title of chapter 4, "A hymn and a secret," recalls Dmitri's first confession to Alyosha in Book III. Even after so much has occurred, Dmitri remains just as concerned about his metaphysical fate; practical considerations continue to be secondary to him. On the day before his trial he exclaims to Alyosha, "It's all over with me" (*BK, 556*). Yet his impending trial, with its probable conviction, does not particularly concern him; the loss of God does.

Here Dostoevsky takes on his favorite old journalistic polemic with the socialists and with social Darwinism, but this time he endows his argument with a new twist—better yet, with a new flick of the tail. Devils and the demonic have already been making their presence felt throughout Book XI; now it is the theories of the nineteenth-century French physiologist Claude Bernard, as espoused by Rakitin, that seek to conquer the battlefield that is Mitya's heart. But Dostoevsky humorously has Mitya recast Bernard's arguments into a framework that fits the increasing presence of the demonic in the novel: "Imagine: inside, in the nerves . . . (damn them!) there are sort of little tails, the little tails of those nerves . . . when they quiver, then an image appears . . . —devil take the moment! . . . That's why I see and then think, because of those tails, not at all because I've got a soul. . . . I am sorry to lose God! It's chemistry, brother, chemistry" (*BK, 557*). In this scheme, guilt and responsibility are reduced to mere chemical reactions.

Moreover, Mitya tells Alyosha that Rakitin, true socialist that he has now become, plans to prove in his forthcoming article that Mitya "couldn't help murdering his father, he was corrupted by his environment. . . . He is going to put in a tinge of socialism" (*BK, 557*). The scene reels with comedy, yet through it Dostoevsky once again underscores his old quarrels with the socialists. He had long believed that the logical outcome of their system, particularly when it excluded God, could be expressed in Ivan's tag phrase, "everything is permitted."

The hymn that Mitya at last sounds forth to Alyosha expresses Mitya's epiphanic dream of the babe as well as the novel's epigraph. The seed has taken root in Mitya; the "new man" hidden within him has "come to the surface" because of the cruel burden that has been placed upon him (*BK*, 560). And as a "new man," Mitya dreams, in messianic fashion, of putting this same mechanism into motion in others—in his future fellow convicts in Siberia.

Dostoevsky here draws on his euphoric letter to his brother on the eve of his own departure to Siberia over 30 years earlier. He had written a letter full of hope:

> Brother, I have not lost courage and I do not feel dispirited. Life is life everywhere, life is within ourselves and not in externals. There will be people around me, and to be a *man* around men, to remain so forever, and not to lose hope and give up, however hard things may be—that is what life is, that is its purpose. . . . Never before have such rich and healthy reserves of spiritual life been seething in me as now. But will my body stand the ordeal?—that I do not know. . . . Life is a gift, life is happiness, each minute could be an eternity of bliss. (*Letters*, 51–53)

Mitya's optimism rings with the same lofty, idealistic cadences as he imagines Siberia. "One may resurrect and revive a frozen heart in that convict . . . one may bring forth an angel. . . . There are so many of them, and we are all responsible for them. . . . It's for the babe I'm going. Because we are all responsible for all. For all the 'babes,' for there are big children as well as little children" (*BK*, 560). Rakitin's social Darwinism removes guilt and responsibility as vital terms in any equation describing human life; Mitya here restores both terms. In seeking to embrace responsibility "for all," he is willing to accept guilt as well.

But his "secret," his plan for a possible escape to America, counterbalances his hymn. (In Dostoevsky's canon, going to America always stands for a negative, godless, vain solution to complex problems.) Could Mitya embrace guilt and responsibility in the role of escaped convict? When Mitya first confessed to Alyosha, he was at a literal as well as figurative crossroad in his life; once again, in Book XI, two alternatives loom before him. As in Book III, his love for Grushenka and his desire to act in an ethical and moral way seem to be at odds with each other. "Sign me with the cross," he begs Alyosha, "for the cross I have to bear tomorrow" (*BK, 565*). He has found himself at a metaphysical crossroad once again. As before, he is fortified by Alyosha, who now passionately asserts his belief that Mitya is not guilty of the murder.

The interrelationship between guilt and responsibility becomes far more complex in chapter 5, when Alyosha finally manages to catch up with Ivan. The tenor of Book XI changes quickly as they stand— also at a key crossing for each of them—beneath the lamppost after leaving Katerina Ivanovna's. Dostoevsky gives this scene a painterly quality: a Rembrandt-like chiaroscuro prevails. Alyosha seeks to inject light into the increasing darkness of Ivan's despair and encroaching madness. The lamppost illuminates the darkness and their pale faces; it shows any viewer as much about the bleakness of the dark as about the power of light.

Ivan's soul hangs in the balance. The devil ("Do you know he visits me?") and God (through his emissary, Alyosha—"God has sent me") wage a battle over it, just as darkness competes with the light in this scene. The question at hand, as in the preceding chapters, is one about guilt. "You have accused yourself and have confessed to yourself that you are the murderer and no one else. But you didn't do it: you are mistaken: you are not the murderer" (*BK, 570*). Alyosha has taken upon himself the responsibility of convincing Ivan that he is not guilty. He has thus, on this crucial day before the trial, shown each of his brothers, accused as they are in different ways—one by society, one by himself—that he believes in their innocence. He has become, literally, his brothers' keeper.

Ivan, continuing in his role of visitor, sets out to visit Smerdyakov for the third time. Taken together, his three visits to Smerdyakov constitute a descent into the most complex aspects of guilt explored in this novel. Chapters 6, 7, and 8 explore the borderline between merely wishing for a criminal act to occur and actually being an accomplice to or instigator of it. The finely tuned psychological probing that goes on in these chapters finds an equally complex juxtaposition in the portrayal of the devil in chapter 9. What is his role in persuading Ivan toward evil?

As twentieth-century readers, we tend to squirm at any demonic interpretations of events if we sense that we are being asked to take them literally. But our modern aesthetic squeamishness cannot undo the fact that Dostoevsky believed in the devil. As a major novelist of the nineteenth century, however, he knew that his readers would balk at the sudden introduction of the devil into a novel that had hitherto operated within the confines of realism, however "fantastic." Dostoevsky's aesthetic sense would not allow him to upset the delicate balance in his novel between religion (the struggle of God and the devil in the heart of man) and psychological motivation. Hence, even as the religious and psychological strands of the novel intensify, their perfect, though competing, balance remains intact.

As Ivan heads off for his third visit to Smerdyakov, the narrator-chronicler backtracks to Ivan's first visit. Ivan had first visited Smerdyakov in the hospital, five days after Fyodor's murder and on the first day of his own arrival back from Moscow. Just before visiting Smerdyakov, Ivan had visited Mitya in prison. This encounter had strengthened Ivan's conscious belief in Mitya's guilt. Nevertheless, the first time he gave evidence to the district prosecutor he had remained silent about his conversation with Smerdyakov just before the murder. Ivan's habit of putting things off has drastic consequences, particularly as Book XI progresses.

In their first conversation, Smerdyakov confuses Ivan by presenting him with a tangle of facts tempered by lies. Smerdyakov interprets their fateful conversation at the gate as a justification of his own innocence. He acknowledges his comment, "It's always worthwhile speaking to a clever man," but asserts that he had not meant it in praise of Ivan but as a reproach. He claims that he had wanted Ivan to go to Chermashnya, not Moscow, so that Ivan would be nearer in case of trouble. Even as he spews out these lies, however, Smerdyakov is uncomfortably aware that God may be listening in. "No one hears this talk of ours now, except Providence itself" (*BK*, 577).

Their first interview ends with a second instance of Ivan deciding, fatally, to remain silent. " 'Goodbye. But I won't say anything of your being able to sham a fit, and I don't advise you to, either,' something made Ivan say suddenly" (*BK*, 577). Smerdyakov concurs and vows a silence of his own that Ivan quickly realizes is insulting. Yet again, he resists his impulse to go back and confront Smerdyakov. Book X had closed with the invocation of Psalm 137, with its emphasis on memory. Here in Book XI Ivan strives toward a dangerous forgetfulness. "He felt as though he wanted to make haste to forget something" (*BK*, 578).

Two weeks after this first interview Ivan finds himself, despite his drive toward forgetfulness, at the mercy of undesired memories, memories that have perhaps surfaced, according to the precept of Zosima, "at the needed time." As Ivan is remembering, with repulsion, the words he had muttered to himself on the train to Moscow—"I am a scoundrel"—he suddenly meets Alyosha. For the first time Ivan lets himself explore that dangerous boundary between the passive desire for evil and the role of accomplice. " 'Tell me, did you think I desired father's death or not?' 'I did think so,' answered Alyosha softly." Then Ivan asks him an even more difficult question: he asks whether Alysoha thought him "prepared to bring that about?" Alyosha turns pale and remains silent. After Ivan has begged for the truth, he at last replies, "Forgive me, I did think that too, at the time" (*BK*, 579). This exchange recalls the ending of Ivan's narrative of the Grand Inquisitor. Then too Alyosha had turned pale as he acknowledged a truth painful for him to utter. Now the chapter that begins with Ivan being persuaded of Mitya's guilt closes with Alyosha's acknowledgment that he had imagined Ivan capable of conspiring in murder. Upon hearing these words, Ivan heads off immediately for his second interview with Smerdyakov.

During the ensuing two weeks, moreover, Ivan's own sense of his guilt has grown. He angrily asks Smerdyakov, "Have I entered into some kind of compact with you?" (*BK*, 581). He asks this even as he denies that he could have known of the murder. Ironically, it is Alyosha whom the demonic Smerdyakov echoes when he accuses Ivan of having desired his father's death. These words, coming from Smerdyakov rather than from Alyosha, provoke Ivan's fury; he strikes Smerdyakov. Despite this dramatic confrontation and Ivan's sudden accusation ("It was you who murdered him!"), Dostoevsky does not yet let these powerful disclosures take root (*BK*, 582). Once again Ivan fatally delays going to the district prosecutor. He rushes instead to Katerina Ivanovna.

He expresses his fear to her. "If it's not Dmitri, but Smerdyakov who's the murderer, I share his guilt, for I put him up to it" (*BK*, 585). His words frighten her into showing him the drunken, self-incriminating letter Mitya had written to her on the first night of the novel's action. The chapter closes with Ivan being more certain than ever that Mitya committed the crime. The seed of truth that had so tentatively planted itself in Ivan has quickly been encased in a husk of verisimilitudinous falsehood and "mathematical proof" (*BK*, 586).

As chapter 8 opens, the reader must take note that chapters 6 and 7 have been chronological backtrackings on the part of the narrator-chronicler. The novel now reenters its ongoing time, that of the day before the trial is to begin. Ivan heads off through the dark for his third and final interview with Smerdyakov. But Alyosha has just spoken his words to Ivan beneath the lamppost; he has softly intoned that God has sent him to tell Ivan that, despite his self-accusation, he is not the murderer. Alyosha makes a firm distinction between desiring and enacting murder. To him those boundaries are clear.

The narrator-chronicler uses every possible device to highlight the importance of Ivan's third visit to Smerdyakov. He carefully prepares for it by his flashback depiction of the first two visits. The chapter title, "The third and last interview with Smerdyakov," also underlines its importance. Even the weather plays a role: as Ivan moves away from the light and Alyosha and toward the darkness and Smerdyakov, he is "unconscious of the storm" (*BK,* 588). Finally, the chapter itself contains a frame and as such is like a short story embedded within the novel. The frame story, moreover, duplicates in miniature the larger drama that Ivan is enacting.

The frame tale concerns a drunken peasant who is singing an uncannily apt ditty, "Ach, Vanka's gone to Petersburg, / I won't wait till he comes back" (*BK,* 588). Ivan feels an automatic hatred for this peasant, who lurches against him. As the peasant falls to the ground, Ivan thinks to himself, "He will freeze." At this point, Ivan, the passionate, theoretical opponent of any system built on unjustified suffering, is in fact ready, even eager, to let a fellow human being die. At the end of the chapter, however, Ivan's second meeting with the peasant serves as a concrete indicator of the change that, however tentatively, has inexorably begun to take place within him. He leaves Smerdyakov with a sense of joy and "unbounded resolution"—a firm hope of putting an end to the "wavering that had so tortured him of late" (*BK,* 600). This time it is Ivan who lurches against the peasant, who is still lying unconscious on the snowy earth. Ivan raises him and saves his life.

Yet these preliminary indications of a spiritual conversion do not yet take firm root. Again Ivan falls victim to that dreaded wavering; again, fatally, he puts off going to the prosecutor. "Everything together tomorrow" (*BK,* 601). His joy vanishes; he enters his room; his eyes fix on one point, and Ivan begins his nightmare encounter with the devil. But the drunken peasant, like all the vital symbols in the novel, exhibits both a positive and a negative valence.[4] He has simultaneously served to indicate not only the measure of Ivan's spiritual regeneration but the tenacity of his moral despair.

Within the perimeters of this frame tale Ivan has his final and decisive interview with Smerdyakov, where again the heat of hell prevails. Both men have changed physically for the worse in the last month: both are ill, with sunken faces and jaundiced eyes. A month earlier a fully recovered Smerdyakov had been spouting Western views and reading a French phrase book. Now he is reading *The Sayings of the Holy Father Isaac the Syrian.* (Terras and others have noted that many of Zosima's teachings are based on this text [Terras, *Karamazov Companion*, 22–23]. Thus its association here with Smerdyakov suggests many rich ambiguities.)

When the demonic Smerdyakov again uncannily repeats Alyosha's words, "you did not murder him," they carry a completely different import, just as did his repetition of Alyosha's words in the second interview. Alyosha was assuring Ivan of his innocence. Smerdyakov's words connote his guilt. They imply that because Ivan did not carry out the actual deed, he is safe. The knife cuts both ways. The phrase "you did not murder him" functions as both an assurance of innocence and an accusation of guilt, depending on the speaker.

Moments later Smerdyakov at last makes his overt accusation. "You are the real murderer, I was only your instrument." Smerdyakov thus neatly combines his roles of devil and lackey: he plants the idea of murder in Ivan's mind, then he carries it out. Smerdyakov assumes, like the devil in the next chapter, the status of a phantom. Ironically, it is Smerdyakov, in his reply to Ivan, who, as he did earlier, brings in God. "There's no phantom here, but only us two and one other. . . . That third is God himself, sir, Providence, sir" (*BK,* 591).

What is the significance of Smerdyakov's affirmation of God's presence? On the one hand it serves to enhance the morality-play atmosphere of this chapter and the next, in which the forces of evil and good compete for the precious treasure of Ivan's soul. The invocation of God's presence also hints to us that Smerdyakov himself has changed, that even if he has not repented of his crime, he has fallen into irrevocable and loathsome despair. Smerdyakov's words—"He is the third beside us now. Only don't look for him, you won't find him" (*BK,* 591)—chillingly recall those of Ivan when he had told the story of Mary's wanderings through hell. He had described the sinners at the bottom of the burning lake: "Some of them sink to the bottom of the lake so that they can't swim out, and 'these God forgets'—an expression of extraordinary depth and force" (*BK,* 228). Smerdyakov finds himself similarly alone.

Yet even as we see Smerdyakov's desperate isolation, Ivan continues to see in him a phantom-devil. When Smerdyakov fumbles in his stocking to pull out the 3,000 rubles, Ivan seems to fear a more unearthly disclosure—perhaps, as Terras suggests, a cloven hoof (Terras, *Karamazov Companion*, 382). He draws back his fingers from the money "as though from contact with a loathsome reptile" (*BK*, 591). Ivan, despite his encroaching illness, handles himself with surprising grace during this interview. He manages, in a sense, to do the right thing. His words suggest that a godly firmness of purpose has seized him, and that the tormenting wavering to which he has been subject has ceased. "God sees . . . perhaps I, too, was guilty. . . . I will give evidence against myself tomorrow, at the trial. . . . But we'll make our appearance together" (*BK*, 598). Ivan seems to have come to terms with the terrible question of the degree of his own guilt.

Once he leaves Smerdyakov, however, despite his sensations of joy and resolution, despite his newfound compassion for the drunken peasant, the "centre cannot hold"; he puts off action until the morning, and his gladness and self-satisfaction "passed in one instant" (*BK*, 601). Yet even at this dark moment, the narrator-chronicler slyly insinuates a ray of hope for Ivan: all his joy does not pass away, only "almost all." That little onion, that "almost," speaks volumes.

Although it quickly began to provoke outrage among some of his readers, Dostoevsky was extremely proud of chapter 9, "The devil. Ivan Fyodorovich's nightmare." A month before his death Dostoevsky wrote to a doctor friend, "Because of that chapter in *The Karamazovs* (about the hallucination) . . . some have already tried to brand me a reactionary . . . a man who has 'written himself out of his mind.' " He then revealed that he intended to give a "critical analysis" of the chapter in a future number of the *Diary* (*Letters*, 514). Unfortunately, death intervened, and we are left with one riddle that Dostoevsky had in fact intended to answer for us.

We do know, however, that Dostoevsky had consulted with doctors, "several of them," about how to depict the nightmares and hallucinations to which someone with Ivan's symptoms of illness would be subject. I have already quoted part of his letter to Lyubimov, written upon sending off the last five chapters of Book XI. In that letter Dostoevsky goes on to describe the immense pleasure he experienced in writing this controversial chapter: "But why am I telling you all this? You will judge for yourself when you read it. . . . You must, however, forgive me my *devil*. It is only a minor devil and not Satan with his "singed wings." . . . Although I myself think that chapter 9 *could have been omitted,* for some reason or other I *greatly enjoyed* writing it and I don't at all wish to disavow it [Dostoevsky's italics]" (*Letters,* 508–9).

These comments offer, to pharaphase Madame Khokhlakova, a gold mine of insights. Besides claiming, through his queries of doctors, an authenticity for Ivan's symptoms, Dostoevsky also conveys in this letter an ambivalence identical to that in the chapter itself. Ivan cannot decide whether the apparition is real or not. Dostoevsky, likewise, does not take a firm position on the matter. Moreover, he urges Lyubimov— an important reader, to say the least—to judge for himself. Finally, even as Dostoevsky reveals his great pleasure in writing this chapter, he admits that it could have been omitted. This is a curious, even baffling observation, for perhaps no chapter in the novel shows us so much about Ivan. As a chapter, it is comparable in its shock value and revela- tory nature to Stavrogin's confession in *The Possessed* (a chapter that was, in fact, omitted by the censor, and that Dostoevsky, when he later had an opportunity to do so, chose not to restore).

Ivan sits looking persistently at an object on the sofa. He sees a man, "a Russian gentleman of a particular kind," who has pathetic pretensions to fashion and gives off "every appearance of gentility on straitened means"—"a toady." Dostoevsky indulges in comic allegory here, for this devil, though in reduced circumstances, is widely received and is "a gentleman who could be asked to sit down with anyone, though, of course, not in a place of honor" (*BK,* 602).

As the devil and Ivan resume their conversation "from last time," it becomes clear that Ivan is intent on convincing himself that the devil is a hallucination. "It's I, *I myself speaking, not you* [Dostoevsky's italics]." But he also admits his doubt. "Only I don't know whether I was dreaming last time or whether I really saw you" (*BK,* 603, 604). This tension in Ivan reigns throughout the chapter. But the devil has a strategy of his own with which he seeks to manipulate Ivan.

Thus the reader must answer at least three difficult questions. Is the devil a hallucination or not? Is the devil's strategy to reawaken faith in Ivan or to squelch it forever? Is the devil here an agent of evil or is he somehow functioning as a way station on Ivan's path to eventual spiritual regeneration? Each of these questions stands, of course, at the gateway to many others. And if Dostoevsky did not presume to answer them for Lyubimov and his other readers, I cer- tainly shall not. Nevertheless, he does ask them. The greatest aesthetic and moral pleasure for readers consists in answering such questions for themselves. Much has already been written on this chapter; I shall simply highlight for a first-time reader some of the moments that seem to express most fully the complexity of Ivan's encounter with his devil.

Ivan proposes to convince himself that the devil is a hallucination by proving that he is "incapable of saying anything new." "You are myself, myself, only with a different mug. You just say what I am thinking." The devil replies by mocking that earthly Euclidean geometry of justice that Ivan had claimed to prefer to the non-Euclidean one. "You see, like you, I suffer from the fantastic and so I love the realism of earth. Here, with you . . . all is formulated and geometrical, while we have nothing but indeterminate equations!" By seeming to be on his side, the devil mocks the profound meaning of Ivan's earlier, agonized rebellion against God's universe. But even as he ridicules and rehashes Ivan's old idea, the devil startles him with something new, thus forcing Ivan to believe, albeit momentarily, in the devil's own existence. He parodies and rephrases an aphorism from Terence that Ivan had never thought of before. As soon as the devil gains this seeming victory, he leads Ivan in the opposite direction, assuring him that even though he is capable of "original" ideas, "I am only your nightmare, nothing more" (*BK*, 605, 606).

The wavering that has been a hallmark of Ivan's condition throughout reaches its apotheosis here. "You are lying, your aim is to convince me you exist apart and are not my nightmare, and now you are asserting you are a dream" (*BK*, 606). Not unexpectedly, we learn that the devil has adopted a "special method" for dealing with Ivan. Just as Ivan had earlier refused to accept the imposition of a non-Euclidean geometry of justice as an answer to earthly suffering, so too does the devil refuse to use non-Euclidean geometry. He describes his travels through space and time in woefully inadequate and humorous Euclidean terms. Moreover, since he was not dressed properly for such a flight, he has caught a cold.

The devil comically sounds in another key Dostoevsky's own ideas about the importance of man's freedom to choose between good and evil. "I was predestined 'to deny' and yet I am genuinely good-hearted. . . . Well, they've chosen their scapegoat, they've made me write the column of criticism and so life was made possible." The devil in *The Legend of the Grand Inquisitor* offers men miracle, mystery, and authority—all in earthly form. Ivan's devil, though comic, is far more insidious; he claims that he himself is the reason life is possible at all. "We understand that comedy. . . . No, live, I am told, for there'd be nothing without you. There would be no events and there must be events" (*BK,* 609).

But in the midst of the devil's seeming embrace of the virtues of realism and predictable Euclidean geometry, he slyly reinjects, through his plagiarism of a parable invented by Ivan himself, an affirmation of the non-Euclidean, even the authentically miraculous. He tells "the legend about Paradise": the story of the doubting philosopher who, after his death, was sentenced to walk "a quadrillion kilometers in the dark," at which point "the gates of heaven" would open and he would be forgiven. The philosopher refuses to go and lies down across the road for "almost" a thousand years. "And then he got up and went on." Ivan, operating within the framework of Euclidean geometry, laughingly protests that his lying or walking makes no difference, for the walk itself would take a billion years. The devil replies, "Much more than that. . . . But he got there long ago and that's where the story begins" (*BK,* 610, 611).

Ironically, this parable works to reawaken Ivan's faith, yet he also remembers that the story was his own and could not have been invented by the devil. The devil's plagiarism thus supports Ivan's notion of him as a hallucination. The irony thus intensifies, for we see Ivan caught in the mysterious act of unconsciously plagiarizing himself; he draws upon something within himself that had remained hidden but had surfaced, as Zosima would say, at the needed time. The devil's role in this process is obscure, but whether he is real or hallucinatory, he seems to be working to reawaken Ivan's faith.

Ivan cries out that he has not the hundredth part of a grain of faith in him. At this point the devil suddenly reveals his "special method": he is a practitioner of homeopathy, the medical science of effecting cures through applying like to like.[5] He duplicates Ivan's doubts and administers a subtle cure for them. "But you have the thousandth of a grain. Homeopathic doses perhaps are the strongest. Confess that you have faith even to the ten-thousandth of a grain." Then, rapidly contradicting himself, as he had a few moments earlier with the quotation from Terence, the devil suddenly asserts that he told the anecdote about the philosopher in order to "destroy your faith." Again Ivan accuses him of lying (*BK,* 612).

In reply, the devil at last reveals his own system of geometry, his own arithmetic; not surprisingly, it too partakes of the seed imagery that so pervades this novel. "I shall sow in you only a tiny grain of faith and it will grow into an oak tree—and such an oak tree that sitting on it, you will long to enter the ranks of 'the hermit monks!' " The devil reveals the value placed on causing even one such saint to fall: "One such soul, you know, is sometimes worth a whole constellation. We have our arithmetic, you know" (BK, 612, 613). Dostoevsky has thus, through his devil, effected a heady mixing of metaphors—the already familiar metaphors about plagiarism, mathematical certainty, and seeds all fuse together in the devil's words. Dostoevsky has let the devil bring to bear his own most precious bag of tricks, all in the effort to drag Ivan toward a renewal of faith.

As Ivan's descent into brain fever becomes more inexorable, he finds himself locked in yet another struggle to define the nature of evil. At least in his "rebellion" and *The Legend of the Grand Inquisitor* the physiognomy of evil was recognizable. Now Ivan finds himself encountering a devil who, though evil, claims to be ultimately on the side of good. "Mephistopheles declared to Faust that he desired evil, but did only good. Well, he can say what he likes, it's quite the opposite with me." Like the Grand Inquisitor, the devil even cries out that he has a dream of reconciliation with God. "I, too, shall walk my quadrillion" (BK, 614,615). The devil rambles on, punctuating his desire for reunification with God with his opposing desire to bring about the appearance of the man-god, a figure who, throughout Dostoevsky's canon, has always represented the antithesis of God.

The devil's words become more diffuse and hysterical; Ivan begins to tremble all over, and, replicating Luther with his inkstand, he thinks to throw a glass at the devil. The interview suddenly ends with the sound of knocking at the window. As Ivan manages at last to leap up to open his door, he notices that the glass remains on the table and the room is empty. The mood of the fantastic prevails, for a moment, with perfect balance. Ivan, Alyosha, and we, the readers, will all have to exit from it eventually and opt for the prevalence of the real or the marvelous.[6] But in the moments before that necessary exit, the rare and authentic presence of the fantastic hovers in the room and perhaps even in our minds.

The news of Smerdyakov's suicide comes as an anticlimax. What is more baffling, though unremarked by the narrator-chronicler, is that Ivan's report to Alyosha on his encounter with the devil does not correspond to what we have just witnessed. He says that the devil ridiculed his motives for his planned confession at the upcoming trial. He reports that the devil had already told him of Smerdyakov's suicide. Why this disparity between Ivan's encounter, hallucinatory or not, and his account of it? What new riddle is Dostoevsky introducing here? Or is he merely portraying a character whose mind is in the process of disintegration, and who can no longer separate fancy from fancy, let alone fancy from fact?

Or is the devil's homeopathic cure beginning to take place? Certainly, according to the principles of homeopathy, every patient seems, on the surface, to get worse as recovery actually begins. That is because a homeopathic cure begins from the inside and works its way out. Alyosha's interpretation duplicates this notion, which was first introduced into the novel by the devil. Alyosha thinks, "God, in Whom he disbelieved, and His truth were gaining mastery over his heart, which still refused to submit." What is this but a description of a spiritual process of recovery that is proceeding according to the principles of homeopathy? Alyosha makes a vital prediction: "Since Smerdyakov is dead, no one will believe Ivan's evidence, but he will go and give it" (*BK*, 622). Once again, Ivan's predicament recalls that of Zosima's mysterious visitor: authentic confessions are rarely believed. The true confession, in earthly terms, usually seems gratuitous and impotent; these are the deceptive earmarks of its unassailable authenticity.

BOOK XII

Just a few words about Book XII, "A miscarriage of justice." Before the trial even begins, we have already been members of the jury in a more fundamental trial, a trial of all the protagonists. Sentence may already have been passed. Each brother has, in his own way, recognized his own guilt, his own responsibility. Book XII, rather than constituting the genuine trial of any of the brothers, stands as the most extended and satiric scandal scene Dostoevsky ever wrote. "All Russia" watches this spectacle. The Karamazov family squabbles, which erupted in the monastery in the first public scandal of the novel, become fodder for the newspapers of an entire country. Dostoevsky has imperceptibly and deftly expanded the canvas of his novel's action. The title, "A miscarriage of justice," sets the tone for what is to follow. Ironically, this longest book of the novel is the least central to its main plot. Instead, it is the epilogue, which in most novels functions as a kind of afterword, that advances the plot in significant ways.

Just as Dostoevsky consulted doctors for the depiction of Ivan's symptoms of encroaching brain fever, so did he consult two prosecutors while he worked on the scenes of Mitya's trial. Ever ready to engage in journalistic polemic, he also used Book XII to express his dissatisfaction with the legal reforms that had taken place in Russia during the 1860s. "Both the lawyer and the prosecutor are presented by me in part as types of our contemporary court (though not based on anyone specifically) with their morality, liberalism, and view of their task" (*BK*, 768). In fact, V. D. Spasovich, one of the most famous lawyers in Russia and a professor of law at the University of St. Petersburg, was, despite Dostoevsky's denials, the prototype for Fetyukovich (blockhead).[7]

Thus far the novel has probed the religious and moral dimensions of guilt, crime, and punishment. Now at the end, in Book XII, Dostoevsky compresses all these questions into the temporal confines of an ongoing trial in the hope that his readers, even as they smile, will see the inherent limitation of a trial as a mode of arriving at "the truth." Like Dickens, Dostoevsky criticized much about the law and the prevailing judicial system in virtually all his novels.

Mitya has many judges. The ladies, though the vast majority of them believe in his guilt, are "in favor of his being acquitted." Their husbands, for the most part, are "biased against the prisoner" (*BK*, 629). But the most important judges are Mitya's brothers, Katerina Ivanovna, Rakitin, Grigory, the kind old Dr. Herzenstube who had known Mitya since childhood, Grushenka, Fetyukovich (the defense attorney), Ippolit Kirillovich (the prosecutor), the three trial judges, the jury, the narrator-chronicler, and, of course, the reader. The verdicts these many judges reach are varied. Moreover, each judges Mitya within a different context and from a different vantage point, ranging from the romantic interest of the ladies, the desire of the men to see a contest between the prosecutor and the defense attorney, and the psychological interest of the prosecution, to the social interests of the president of the court and the political interpretations of Rakitin.

Dostoevsky injects a note of absurdity into the very possibility of giving an account of the trial by having his narrator-chronicler suddenly become muddled. The narrator-chronicler cannot promise us anything about the accuracy of his own account. "Some things I did not hear, others I did not notice, and others I have forgotten, [and] . . . I have literally no time or space to mention everything that was said or done" (*BK*, 626). After this disclaimer, he proceeds to do just that.

Among the witnesses called to testify, two—Grigory and Dr.

Herzenstube—serve to awaken the jury's compassion through their recollections of Mitya as a child, although each believes in his guilt. Both of them function as stern but just father figures worthy of Mitya's love, which they each receive. In particular, Dr. Herzenstube's anecdote about the pound of nuts underscores yet again the power of the novel's epigraph. Mitya had remembered, for some 23 years, Dr. Herzenstube's gratuitous act of kindness to him as a child when the doctor had given him some nuts. Mitya had quite recently come to thank him. Both had then shed tears together, and as Dr. Herzenstube tenderly tells the story in the courtroom, Mitya weeps again. "And I am weeping now, German, I am weeping now, too, you saintly man" (*BK*, 641).

Dr. Herzenstube's story recalls Mitya's own dream of the babe, yet the babe here is the neglected child Mitya, who may suddenly be linked in the reader's mind with Alexey, the dead child of the grieving peasant woman at the beginning of the novel, and with the dying Ilyusha, whom Mitya has himself wronged. This linkage occurs through the narrator-chronicler's powerful evocation of detail. We recall the details about the three-year-old Alexey and about Ilyusha, and now Dr. Herzenstube projects a similarly detailed and heart-rending image of the toddler Mitya: "Oh, I remember him very well, a little chap so high, left neglected by his father in the backyard, when he ran about without boots on his feet, and his little breeches hanging by one button" (*BK*, 640).

As we might expect, Alyosha's evidence helps Mitya, but Katerina Ivanovna, though initially seeming to help, ends by hurting him. "Katya, why have you ruined me?" (*BK*, 647). With Alyosha's testimony we see Dostoevsky as the expert mystery writer, for Alyosha's sudden recollection, his evidence about Mitya striking his chest at a point too high up to really be his chest—corroborating Mitya's own story of the "little bag" with 1,500 rubles in it—is fully consistent with those events at the beginning of the novel: " 'You see, here, here—there's terrible disgrace in store for me.' (As he said 'here,' Dmitri Fyodorovich struck his chest with his fist with a strange air, as though the dishonor lay precisely on his chest, in some spot, in a pocket, perhaps, or hanging around his neck)" (*BK*, 143). This detailed foreshadowing is particularly interesting given that the novel appeared serially.

Indeed, until Ivan takes the stand the trial seems to be proceeding with a reasonable amount of evidence coming forth in Mitya's favor.

The affection of Grigory and Dr. Herzenstube, the drunkenness of Grigory on the night of the murder, the innkeeper Trifon Borisovich's dishonesty about money, Rakitin's discrediting as a hostile witness, Alyosha's sudden recollection of Mitya's oddly aimed gesture of striking himself on the chest, and Katerina Ivanovna's claim that she did not expect the money to be repaid right away, and even her story of their first encounter—all these disclosures would seem to be potentially helpful to Mitya's case.

But in this strange trial the truth, as Mitya quickly realizes during Katerina Ivanovna's first round of testimony, serves to damage his case. Ivan's sudden producing of the stolen money and his accusation of Smerdyakov and himself ("Who doesn't desire his father's death?") hurts Mitya most of all. Moreover, like Grushenka and Alyosha, Ivan, when he speaks the truth, has no proof of it. "That's just it. I have no proof" (*BK*, 652). The court reacts to Ivan as the mysterious visitor's interlocutors did to him so long ago.

Yet to us Ivan's words summarize the immense spiritual journey he has undergone. His wavering has continued until the last moment: he has approached, departed from, and reapproached the witness stand. Although his words sound like mad ramblings to those in the courtroom, to us they have a poetic and recapitulative significance. At last he cries out: "You see, listen to me. I told him I don't want to keep quiet and he talked about the geological cataclysm . . . idiocy! Come, release the monster . . . he's been singing a hymn. . . . It's like a drunken man in the street bawling how 'Vanka went to Petersburg,' and I would give a quadrillion quadrillion for two seconds of joy" (*BK*, 652). By the time a hysterical Katerina Ivanovna, intent on saving Ivan, offers up her "mathematical proof" of Mitya's guilt, we know that all is lost for Mitya. The devil's arithmetic seems operative in the courtroom.

We have seen at length Mitya's extraordinary skill at creating and depicting possible scenarios of action for himself, beginning with his description of his successive motivations in his first meeting with Katerina Ivanovna. Now his drunken letter to her, describing yet another of his unexecuted plans, is interpreted as evidence for what actually occurred. His own character, his habit of working out innumerable scenarios before settling on a single course of action, has undone him. Katerina Ivanovna shrieks, "Look, everything is written there beforehand, just as he committed the murder after. The whole scenario" (*BK*, 655). The dreadful irony of this scene is that, to defend

Ivan, Katerina Ivanovna makes her consummate accusation of Mitya at the very moment when she believes "all of a sudden" that it is Ivan who is guilty.

In Books X and XI Dostoevsky had sounded in a variety of keys the interrelated questions of the determination of one's own guilt and one's own responsibility. Here in Book XII, however, the action focuses on the question of how one can judge the guilt of another. The prosecutor's speech, his "swan song," offers an astute summation of each of the members of the Karamazov family and an analysis of them in terms of contemporary Russian problems. Fyodor was a "typical father of today"; Ivan's "Europeanism" is described, as is Alyosha's "return to [the] native soil"; Mitya himself "seems to represent Russia directly" (*BK*, 661, 662, 663).

Indeed, the prosecutor's speech ironically forecasts what has been the shape of much subsequent commentary on the novel, even though all the specific conclusions he draws are wrong. His ideas represent a peculiar, yet powerful blend of fact and fancy; he draws precisely the wrong conclusions from shrewd, correct initial premises and deductions about Mitya's character. Particularly sharp is his agreement with Dr. Varvinsky that Mitya has been in his right mind all long. He makes the indisputable point that none of those who believe Smerdyakov to be guilty—Mitya, Ivan, Alyosha, and Grushenka—have been able to provide a single fact to support the idea.

Both the prosecutor and the defense attorney shrewdly use the tools of psychology to scrutinize the facts, and each brilliantly misinterprets them. Ippolit Kirillovich, for example, understands that Dmitri "can contemplate two extremes and both at once" (*BK*, 682), but he then consistently identifies the wrong extreme as the one chosen. He fails, in his psychological reasoning, to suppose that Smerdyakov might have lied to Mitya about where the envelope was hidden, and he thus falls neatly into Smerdyakov's psychological trap: he maintains that the presence of the torn envelope on the floor proves that it could not have been taken by Smerdyakov, who, knowing what the envelope contained, would have had no reason to rip it open at the scene of the crime.

The blend of fact and fancy in the case for the defense is a different one. As Fetyukovich begins his speech, we can agree with his initial premise: "There is an overwhelming chain of evidence against the defendant, and at the same time not one fact that will stand criticism if it is examined separately" (*BK*, 689). Moreover, in attacking the prosecutor, Fetyukovich utters a truth that has been axiomatic throughout the novel: "But profound as psychology is, it's a knife that cuts both ways." He praises the prosecutor's canny citation of the "broad Karamazov nature" and "the two extreme abysses which a Karamazov can contemplate at once" (*BK*, 690) and then uses his own psychological knife to carve out a completely different hypothesis about Mitya: that he did not steal the money, that he did keep 1,500 rubles sewn up in a bag, and, in the first part of his argument at least, that he did not commit the murder.

His analysis of Smerdyakov, in which he scrutinizes the agonizing difference between despair and penitence, is the most accurate that we have had so far. He suggests that in Smerdyakov's guilty suicide we see only the former. Moreover, he paints an accurate portrait of Mitya's character and shows him to be a man undone by his tendency—as in the drunken letter to Katerina Ivanovna—to create vivid scenarios. Dostoevsky seems to agree with Fetyukovich here that Mitya's fate lies hidden in his own character. This view of character as fate—as opposed to the classical notion of fate being determined by the gods—is a profoundly Shakespearean one. As we know, Dostoevsky, like both his fictional prosecutor and defense attorney, knew his Shakespeare well.

In fact, Fetyukovich's view of the real events lying behind Fyodor's murder comes closest to Dostoevsky's own, until the crucial moment when Fetyukovich's argument veers sharply away and gives itself up to an absurd self-destructiveness. We know by now that Dostoevsky typically gives some of his own views to characters whose ideas he ultimately ridicules and repudiates. Fetyukovich becomes a true blockhead, for at the moment when he should have concluded his argument, he launches instead into a theoretical justification for negating filial bonds. "Filial love for an unworthy father is an absurdity." He then denies the mystical bond that exists only *on faith* between parents and children; he argues that parental love must be earned, that its bases are "rational, responsible and strictly humanitarian" (*BK*, 706, 708).

His argument reads as a dangerously reductive version of Ivan's ideas. Moreover, he suddenly retraces the events of the fateful night of the murder and suggests, that if, even though he does not believe it, Mitya *did* in fact kill Fyodor, the act was an unpremeditated gesture of "indignant disgust"; and that he had not meant to kill his father. "Such a murder," Fetyukovich concludes preposterously, "is not a murder. Such a murder is not a parricide" (*BK*, 709). Fetyukovich has effectively unraveled his own defense. Earlier he had ridiculed the prosecutor for claiming to argue in Mitya's defense; here Fetyukovich foolishly and unwittingly wins the case for the prosecution.

Mitya stands accused by both sides, by the best that the temporal judicial system can muster. The muddle is complete. Mitya stands up and declares his innocence. It is time for the jury to reach its verdict. Given the evidence and the spectacle with which they have been presented, it is no surprise that, after a mere hour's deliberation, "the peasants stand firm" (*BK*, 711) and declare him guilty.

THE EPILOGUE

A radiant fellowship of the fallen.
—Joshua Chamberlain

In the deserts of the heart
Let the healing fountain start.
—W. H. Auden

It is my hope that readers, having read the novel—and this introduction to it—up to this point, can simply sit down to a well-earned reading of the epilogue in which its varied levels of meaning, its rhymes, and its symbols can interact in the pleasurable, yet serious *jouissance* that is perhaps the greatest satisfaction to be derived from the experience of reading. Usually the epilogue to a novel serves to separate the reader from the characters, to distance him from the action, and to provide a more or less neutral buffer zone between the world of the novel and the real world that the reader will reenter upon putting down the book. This epilogue completes none of these tasks; its purposes are entirely different. We are drawn more deeply than ever into the action, we are implicated in it, and the zone we enter here is highly charged and anything but neutral.

The theme of memory juts like a vein of golden ore through the epilogue. Alyosha, in his familiar role, moves from Katerina Ivanovna's house to the hospital to Ilyusha's funeral. In each of the three chapters he gives crucial and loving advice, predicated on the belief, derived from Zosima, that memory can shape the future course of a life. He thus begs Katerina Ivanovna to visit Mitya. "Your eyes ought to meet. How will you live all your life, if you don't make up your mind to do it now?" (*BK*, 720). He wholly sanctions the plan for Mitya's escape and offers him a genuine reassurance that is not a rationalization. Along the way, he invokes again the sustaining power of memory: "If you had murdered our father it would grieve me that you should reject your cross. But you are innocent, and such a cross is too much for you. You wanted to make yourself another man by suffering. I say, only remember that other man always, all your life and wherever you escape to; and that will be enough for you" (*BK*, 723).

By the third and final chapter of the epilogue the theme of memory and the vital, ongoing symbols of the novel simultaneously reach their apotheosis. Numbers important to Christian belief also play a role. This epilogue follows 12 earlier books. There are "about twelve" boys; the 12 followers of Alyosha recall the 12 apostles of Jesus. At last there is a death in which, to everyone's surprise—as opposed to their expectation—the corpse does not stink. "Strange to say there was practically no smell from the corpse" (*BK*, 728). And like Markel, so many years before, the dying Ilyusha had thought of the birds.

It is a curious yet meaningful fact that this, the last chapter of fiction Dostoevsky wrote before his death, even as it ties together the many disparate threads of his huge novel—and thus illustrates Zosima's aphorism about all things being connected—should also have a startling resonance with the first story Dostoevsky ever wrote, *Poor People*. There, too, a heartbroken father, like Snegiryov (and like Dostoevsky himself over the death of his son), weeps and, oblivious to the cold weather, loses his hat. As Dostoevsky describes Snegiryov's grief, the abundance of heartrending detail again gives the scene its painful immediacy: the crumpled flowers, Ilyusha's empty bed, his little boots.

Alyosha's words strikingly recall those of Zosima to the peasant woman: "Let them weep," he says (*BK*, 732). Alyosha and the boys approach Ilyusha's stone, where Ilyusha and his father used to come to feed the birds at sunset. Dostoevsky has carefully set the scene for the final tour de force of his novel. Just as *The Idiot* depicts near its end a powerfully conceived verbal icon—a negative one: Myshkin and Rogozhin lie face to face beside the dead Nastasia Filippovna—here, too, we suddenly find ourselves confronted by a haunting icon, one whose terms are, despite the sadness of events, hauntingly optimistic.

Alyosha remembers all that Snegiryov had told him, "the whole picture," and he spontaneously delivers a message to the boys. "Let us make a compact, here at Ilyusha's stone, that we will never forget, first,

Ilyushechka, and second, one another." Alyosha, recalling Jesus with Peter and the apostles, founds his living church, his brotherhood of children by a rock. And their brotherhood is cemented by the very mortar that Ivan had earlier so eloquently refused to accept—the unjustified suffering of a child. "And . . . whatever happens to us later in life . . . let us always remember how we buried the poor boy at whom we once threw stones, do you remember, by the bridge" (*BK*, 733). Those stones and the stone at which Alyosha and the boys stand become a physically embodied spiritual sustenance. For Alyosha and the boys, the stones, as it were, become bread. The boys are all guilty; they have all contributed to Ilyusha's suffering. Yet they accept themselves and their brotherhood, though their edifice does stand upon a child's tears.

In the terms this novel puts forth, a kind of miracle has been wrought, for we, too, forgive these boys, even as Ivan's words about the mother of a tortured child ring in our ears. "The truth is not worth such a price. . . . Let her forgive him for herself. . . . But the sufferings of her tortured child she has no right to forgive" (*BK*, 226). Although Alyosha would not consent then to be "the architect" of such an edifice, he now finds himself in that role: he is the architect, the builder, of precisely such an edifice, to which we, he, and the boys do mutually consent.

In these last magnificent pages, as the boys make their compact founded on memory, words denoting memory and remembrance occur some 30 times. Memories and the very words used to express them become, literally, the seeds that, having died, bear fruit. Alyosha's words echo those of Zosima, those of Grushenka, and, indirectly, even those of the devil when he spoke about faith. Alyosha affirms, "If one has only one good memory left in one's heart, even that may sometimes be the means of saving us" (*BK*, 734). He then bids the boys to remember this moment when they are all remembering Ilyusha and his stone. He forges here a unit of memory that is simultaneously a recollection, and the recollection of a recollection, and which will operate for them in the future as an even more densely layered and sustaining recollection and meta-recollection. An attempt to describe the components of this moment comes dangerously close to linguistic gibberish. In this way, though, the novel resists efforts to reduce it to succinct paraphrase and affirms the value of life over theories about life.

Notes

Chapter 1

1. Simon Karlinsky, ed., *Anton Chekhov's Life and Thought: Selected Letters and Commentary,* trans. Michael Henry Heim, in collaboration with Simon Karlinsky (Berkeley: University of California Press, 1973), 6.

2. Vladimir Nabokov, *Lectures on Russian Literature,* ed. Fredson Bowers (New York: Harcourt Brace Jovanovich, 1981), 6.

Chapter 2

1. Sigmund Freud, "Dostoevsky and Parricide," reprinted in *Dostoevsky: A Collection of Critical Essays,* ed. René Wellek (Englewood Cliffs, N.J.: Prentice-Hall,1962), 98. For a penetrating analysis of the biographical inaccuracies in Freud's essay see Joseph Frank, *Dostoevsky: The Seeds of Revolt 1821–1849* (Princeton: Princeton University Press, 1976), 379–91.

2. Dostoevsky to N. Strakhov, 26 February–10 March 1869, quoted in Donald Fanger, *Dostoevsky and Romantic Realism: A Study of Dostoevsky in Relation to Balzac, Dickens, and Gogol* (Cambridge, Mass.: Harvard University Press, 1965), 218. Fanger cites this letter as part of his larger analysis of Dostoevsky's "fantastic realism" (214–28).

3. Virginia Woolf, "More Dostoevsky," *Times Literary Supplement* (12 February 1917), reprinted in *Books and Portraits: Some further selections from the literary and biographical writings of Virginia Woolf,* ed. Mary Lyon (New York: Harcourt Brace Jovanovich, 1981), 119.